VAN ZORN

THE MACMILLAN COMPANY
NEW YORK · BOSTON · CHICAGO · DALLAS
ATLANTA · SAN FRANCISCO

MACMILLAN & CO., Limited
LONDON · BOMBAY · CALCUTTA
MELBOURNE

THE MACMILLAN CO. OF CANADA, Ltd.
TORONTO

VAN ZORN

A COMEDY IN THREE ACTS

BY

EDWIN ARLINGTON ROBINSON

New York
THE MACMILLAN COMPANY
1928

PRINTED IN THE UNITED STATES OF AMERICA
BY BERWICK & SMITH CO.

TO

HERMANN HAGEDORN

VAN ZORN

CHARACTERS

VAN ZORN

GEORGE LUCAS

WELDON FARNHAM

OTTO MINK

MRS. LOVETT

VILLA VANNEVAR

JENNY

ACT I

ACT I

WELDON FARNHAM'S *studio in Macdougal Alley, New York. In the rear is a long window, beneath which is a wide cushioned seat, extending from the left wall to a vestibule on the right, from which a door, front, opens into the studio. The door is hidden by a tall screen. Further down on the right is another door, and still further down is an antique cabinet, upon which rests a bust of Shakespeare. To the left of the cabinet, well into the room, is a table, upon which are a few books and, among other objects, an ornamental cigar box of polished mahogany. Half way down the left wall, which is built diagonally into the stage, cutting off about one-third of the rear wall, is an open grate with a mantel. Well to the front, on the left, is an upright wheeling easel, upon which a framed portrait faces the rear. There are several chairs, for the most part plain and small; but one of them, near the table, to the left, is large and comfortable.*

The curtain rises, revealing WELDON FARNHAM *and* OTTO MINK. FARNHAM *is a well-conditioned and well-satisfied man of thirty, or a little more, with a certain complacent hardness about his face, which suggests an aggressiveness that does not really exist. He stands surveying* OTTO, *a younger man—short, plump, pink and loquacious—who in turn stands surveying the picture on the easel. His hands are in his trousers pockets, and he stands from time to time on the tips of his toes during the process of his scrutiny.*

FARNHAM
[*As if amused*]

Well, Otto, aren't you going to say something?

3

OTTO

[*Slowly, with a frown*]

So this is Villa Vannevar.*

FARNHAM

Not exactly.   It's a picture of her.

[*Smiling*]

You don't care for it, I see.—Lucas and Petherick think it's rotten.

OTTO

Did Lucas say that?

FARNHAM

[*Still amused*]

No, but he smoked it.   He might as well have said it.

OTTO

[*Leaving the picture and lighting a cigarette*]

You can't always tell what Old Hundred means—when he doesn't say anything.   Or when he does, for that matter.

FARNHAM

[*Smiling*]

I'm sorry, Otto, that you don't like the picture.

OTTO

[*Showing his teeth*]

There's genius in it.   Is that what you wanted me to say?

FARNHAM

But a poor likeness—eh?

———————

* Pronounced Vannee'-vr.

OTTO

Likeness?—Farnham, you make me sick.

[FARNHAM *scowls quickly and laughs*]

I beg your pardon, but you do,—just now, I mean.

[*With a sniff*]

You and your pictures!

FARNHAM

[*Laughing*]

Are they all so bad as that, Otto?

OTTO

[*Irritated*]

I suppose it's *you* that I'm talking about, not your pictures.

FARNHAM

[*With patronage*]

You don't seem to be improving matters very much. What have *I* done?

OTTO

[*With affectionate disgust*]

You? You haven't done anything. Destiny, or something or other, has done it for you.

FARNHAM

[*Laughing*]

But I don't believe much in destiny. I believe in work.

OTTO

You didn't work very hard to get the best girl in New York.

FARNHAM

If I didn't know you, Otto, I might be offended.

[*Laughing*]

What's the matter with you to-day, anyhow?

OTTO

[*With all sincerity*]

I understand. You think I'm jealous, but I'm not. I'm not such a dam fool.

FARNHAM

Otto, don't be so impulsive.

[*He laughs*]

OTTO

Impulsive? You don't know what the word means.

[*With a grimace*]

You might at least look glad, or say something foolish once in a while,—just to let a fellow know that you're human.

FARNHAM

[*Seriously*]

I'll take back a part of what I said, Otto. There may be a large element of destiny in my—we'll say my very great good fortune.

[*Laughing*]

But I wouldn't say as much as that to Van Zorn.

OTTO

Van Zorn? He's a fatalist, isn't he?

FARNHAM
[Laughing]

I don't know just what he is. He's the best man living, and he's my best friend.

OTTO
[Cheerfully]

And he's worth about how many millions?

FARNHAM
[With animation]

I don't know. Twenty or twenty-five. I don't care much about that part of it.

OTTO

You know, Farnham, I believe you when you say that.
[Moving to the Right]

If I didn't, I shouldn't hang around your place any more. You think you wouldn't miss me if I didn't, but you would. I'm a tender shoot, and I'm delicate, and you'll be dam sorry when I'm dead.

[OTTO *pauses before the bust of Shakespeare, looks at it thoughtfully, places his hat upon it carefully, and surveys the result with satisfaction.* FARNHAM *watches him with patronizing amusement. Presently, when the two men stand looking at each other, the bell rings*]

FARNHAM
[Looking at his watch]

That sounds like Lucas. It can't be Mrs. Lovett—yet.

OTTO

It's Old Hundred, I'll bet a sequin. Let him in.

[FARNHAM *admits* GEORGE LUCAS, *who is a square-jawed and somewhat cadaverous looking man of thirty, with a melancholy and highly intellectual face. His clothes are well kept, but unmistakably the worse for wear, and there is a whimsical weariness in his manner that might be suggestive of latent tragedy. He looks at* FARNHAM *and* OTTO *as if he expected them to say something*]

OTTO

Good morning, Phœbus-Apollo.

LUCAS

[*With a benignant smile*]

Good morning.

[*To* FARNHAM, *half quizzically*]

Good morning.

[*He looks at the decorated bust of Shakespeare, and then at* OTTO. *He smiles once more and removes his hat, which* FARNHAM *takes and tosses on to window-seat*]

OTTO

Have you come to join the celebration?

LUCAS

Celebration of what?

OTTO

Oh, I don't know. You take your choice. You might celebrate the publication of my new book, or you might celebrate the rotation of the planet Neptune—on his axis. Or, you might celebrate the engagement of our friend Farnham to the radiant Miss Villa Vannevar.

[*Motioning towards the picture*]
There she is—or, I should say, a picture of her.

LUCAS
[*With gathering surprise and difficulty*]
I have seen the picture, but I had not heard of the engagement.
[*Giving his hand to* FARNHAM, *but as if with unconscious reluctance*]
Farnham, let me congratulate you.

FARNHAM
[*Taking his hand*]
Thank you, Lucas.
[*As* LUCAS *goes towards the picture*]
I fear that some of us get rather more than we deserve in this life.

LUCAS
[*Affecting indifference*]
Oh, I don't know about that.
[*Studying the picture*]
So this is Villa Vannevar.

OTTO
[*Promptly, with his hands in his pockets*]
That's what *I* said.

FARNHAM
[*Comfortably*]
Your congratulations are quite enough, Lucas. You needn't feel obliged to praise the picture.

LUCAS

[*Solemnly*]

I wasn't going to praise the picture.

OTTO

[*Standing on his toes and grinning at* FARNHAM *with satisfaction*]

"Heaven is not reached with a single bound." You can't have everything at once, Farnham, even if you are a genius. But you might give Lucas a drink, and you might give me a bottle of cold beer.

FARNHAM

[*Amused*]

In the morning, Otto? Isn't this something new?

OTTO

[*Nodding at the bust*]

Shakespeare did it, and I wish to do everything that Shakespeare did—so far as in me lies.

FARNHAM

[*Laughing, as if* OTTO *were a child*]

Well, all right, if I've got it.

[*He goes out at the right,* LUCAS *leaves the picture, frowning to himself, and returns to* OTTO, *who is standing near the corner of the vestibule.* OTTO *turns* LUCAS *gently and assists him towards the cabinet, from which* LUCAS *takes out a bottle of whiskey and a glass, going with them to the table nearby.* FARNHAM *returns with a bottle of beer and a glass*]

FARNHAM

[*After a look at* LUCAS]

Here you are, Stratford.

[OTTO *goes to the window seat*]

Don't you want some water, Lucas?

LUCAS

No, thank you. It won't be necessary.

FARNHAM

[*With mild insistence*]

Better for the heart.

OTTO

[*Prying the cap from the bottle*]

Lucas hasn't got any heart.

[*He pours out a glass of beer with care*]

Well, Farnham, you man of iron, *morituri salutamus*. I'm a tender shoot, and I shan't be with you very long. Neither will Lucas, if he doesn't drink some water one of these days.

[*There is a sinister note in his last words, and it is evidently caught by the other men*]

LUCAS

[*With a dry flourish*]

Farnham, you are a man of parts, and once more I congratulate you. I'm a man of parts myself, as a matter of fact, but some of my parts don't exactly fit, and as a consequence

[*With a hard, insincere laugh*]

as a consequence, I—I rattle. Your health and happiness.

[*He drinks, and shivers a little*]

And now,

[Exploring the table]

If you will give me a small cigar

[He takes a large one from the box]

I'll tell you what a great man you are going to be.

[He puts back the bottle and moves again towards the picture]

FARNHAM

[Who has been watching LUCAS *with a patronizing smile]*

And now if you two fellows will kindly make yourselves at home, I'll be back in a little while. I'm going over to Petherick's to get some photographs of his comical bust of Poe for Mrs Lovett; and if anyone comes in while I'm gone, I'll trust you two to be agreeable.

LUCAS

[Nervously]

But what does this mean, Farnham? If you expected visitors, why didn't you say so?

FARNHAM

[Soothingly]

They are coming to see the picture in its new frame.

[Hesitating]

Of course you remember Mrs. Lovett—and Villa Vannevar?

LUCAS

[In a dry voice]

Yes, I remember them. Villa Vannevar and I used to be rather good friends.

[Indifferently]

But I doubt if Mrs Lovett remembers me.

FARNHAM
[*At the door*]

She must.

LUCAS
[*Sitting down*]

Why do you say that?

FARNHAM

She must,—for you are not the kind that women forget.
[*He laughs and goes out, and* LUCAS *follows him with his eyes.
He remains for a time as if in retrospection*]

OTTO
[*From the window seat, after a pause*]

It seems to me that Farnham might have done a little
better than that.

[LUCAS *gives him a quick look*]

But I don't know,

[*In half soliloquy*]

perhaps he couldn't, after all.

[OTTO *studies the beer-bottle as if it were a rare vase, and* LUCAS,
*leaning forward on his chair, rubs his fingers together thought-
fully.*

OTTO

Phœbus,

[LUCAS *looks at him*]

wake up.

LUCAS

I am awake.

OTTO

The devil you are.

[Getting up and stretching himself]

Let's have another look at Farnham's picture.   Petherick
thinks it's rotten.

[Mercifully]

But then, Petherick's a sculptor.

LUCAS

[Drily]

Can't sculptors tell when things are rotten?

OTTO

[Briskly]

Apparently not—if we are to judge them by what they
have done for our fair city.

LUCAS

[Rising and smiling]

You are severe this morning, Otto.

[In a fatherly way]

I hope you aren't going to be severe with *me*.

OTTO

[Looking at him sharply]

I *was* going to be—but I won't now.

[Frowning before the picture]

So this is Villa Vannevar.

LUCAS

[Smiling]

That's what *I* said.

OTTO

[*Still frowning*]

Mrs. Weldon Farnham.

[*Throwing up his hands*]

Lucas, I can't make it sound right.

LUCAS

[*Drily*]

What's wrong about the sound of it?   Farnham is a good fellow, isn't he?

OTTO

[*With emphasis*]

He's a fine fellow; and he's one of his own best friends.

LUCAS

[*Smiling grimly*]

Well, that makes for prudence—and for longevity.

OTTO

[*Drily*]

Very good indeed.   What do you think of this picture, Phœbus, anyhow?

LUCAS

It's a pretty good picture.   All things are relative.

OTTO

[*Promptly*]

Then you agree with Petherick.

LUCAS

Not necessarily.

[*He looks around him uncomfortably*]

But I don't believe, Otto, that I'll stay here any longer.

[OTTO *moves toward him*]

You can entertain these women without me.

OTTO

[*Backing* LUCAS *into his chair*]

There! You try that for a while. Farnham said you were to stay here till he came back.

[*He takes another chair and sits facing* LUCAS]

Phœbus, you may kick me if you like, but I'm sorry for you. I'm dam sorry.

LUCAS

[*With a doubtful scowl*]

What do you think you are talking about, Otto?

OTTO

[*Plunging*]

Phœbus, I like you. I like you a lot. I've liked you for ten years—ever since I met you.

[*Pause*]

So far as I count for anything, I suppose I'm as good a friend as you have in the world.

LUCAS

[*Pleased and embarrassed*]

I'm glad to hear you say that, Otto.

OTTO

[*With more confidence*]

You'd better wait till I'm done with you.

LUCAS

[*Smiling*]

Go on. I'm at your service.

OTTO

[*Clasping his knee and becoming very serious*]

Very well. Tell me when to stop.

[*Pause*]

Phœbus, how much does Farnham know about you?
Did he know anything about you before he came to
New York? Let me see, that was four years ago.

LUCAS

[*Surprised*]

Probably not.

OTTO

Well, then, did Farnham know Villa Vannevar before
he came to New York?

LUCAS

[*Surprised*]

Not to my knowledge.

OTTO

Am I getting too personal?

LUCAS

[*Fighting with his curiosity*]

You haven't said anything injurious.

OTTO

Good. Now does Farnham . . . Oh, the devil! I
suppose I ought not to ask you this, but I'm going to, all

the same.   Does Farnham know that Villa Vannevar cared more for you at one time than she cares now for any other man living?

LUCAS

[*Rubbing his hands slowly*]

I rather think, Otto, that you may as well stop.

OTTO

Are you going to kick me?

LUCAS

No.   Your motive is good, and I try to judge a fellow by his motive.

[*Taking a cheap watch from his pocket, he looks at it and shakes it at his ear*]

What time is it?

OTTO

[*With much vigor*]

Phœbus, you can't put me off.   I've got you now, and I'm going to tell you what I think of you.

LUCAS

[*Shaking his watch at his ear*]

What do you think of me?

OTTO

[*Nettled*]

Well, I think you are going to the devil, for one thing.

LUCAS

[*Grinning*]

Only going?   I was told the other day that I had arrived—with banners.

OTTO

Did Farnham tell you that?

LUCAS

That was Farnham's hidden meaning.

OTTO

[*After a pause*]

Well, Phœbus, I can't speak for Farnham. But there
was a time when the rest of us would have said that you
had empires up your sleeve.

[*Impressively*]

LUCAS

[*Looking at his sleeve*]

Then they must be there yet. I've never shaken them
out.

OTTO

[*With more fervor*]

They may be there, but all the devils in hell, with
microscopes, couldn't find them there this morning. As
you are fond of reading, you may have gathered, from
various authorities, that empires don't run themselves,
exactly. When they do, they run down.

LUCAS

Like my watch.

[*He shakes it, and returns it to his pocket*]

OTTO

[*Getting up with a sigh*]

Phœbus, why don't you try to find out where you are,

and stop pickling your brain with rum, and quit be-
wildering your inferiors, and go back to school? If you
don't, there will be a funeral one of these days, and you
won't have to walk. And what I say is all as true as God
made great whales and little squirrels.

LUCAS

[*Rubbing his knees and grinning*]

Good. Say on.

[OTTO *gives a snort of disgust and moves towards the bust of
Shakespeare, his hands in his trousers' pockets and his face
puckered with a scowl*]

LUCAS

[*Watching* OTTO *with weary amusement*]

Otto, tell me something more about this much-travelled
Odysseus of many devices, whom Farnham calls Van
Zorn.

[OTTO *removes his hat from the bust*]

I thought you would do that, Otto.

[OTTO *puts his hat on his head and gives* LUCAS *a look of
discouragement*]

Tell me about Van Zorn, Otto, and take off your hat.

[OTTO *spins his hat at* LUCAS, *who catches it deftly and throws it
over to the window seat*]

I understand that he's a fatalist—or something or other.
Where does he live?

OTTO

[*Piqued*]

He doesn't live anywhere. He doesn't have to. He's
worth about twenty-five millions.

LUCAS

That isn't very much.   Is he in town?

OTTO

[*Impatiently*]

Yes, he's in town.

LUCAS

How long is he going to stay?

OTTO

[*Wearily*]

How the devil do I know?   I suppose he'll stay as long as he likes the place.   That's what I should do, if I had twenty-five millions.

[*Becoming more rancid*]

And then, if the fancy seized me, I should pack my suitcase and go in for the irrigation of Mesopotamia.

LUCAS

[*Still leaning forward and rubbing his hands slowly*]

When is Farnham to be married?

OTTO

I don't know.   Didn't you hear about the engagement?

LUCAS

[*Getting up and speaking without apparent interest*]

No . . . I don't hear about things any more.

[*The bell rings and* LUCAS *turns with a start*]

I wonder who that is.

[*He takes his watch from his pocket nervously and pretends to look at it*]

OTTO

[*Smiling as he looks at his own watch*]

If you wish to know what time it is, it's five minutes to twelve.

[OTTO *opens the door and admits* MRS. LOVETT *and* MISS VILLA VANNEVAR. MRS. LOVETT *is a short lady of fifty, with a manner that is slightly affected, but not comically so. She is dressed in black, and in a manner calculated to suggest rather than to express mourning.* VILLA VANNEVAR *is rather tall and very handsome, inclined to be unconventional and at times careless, naturally vivacious, but evidently not satisfied with her existence. She wears a walking suit of bright gray, with a smart hat*]

OTTO

[*With familiar mock-ceremony*]

You are to come in—both of you—and you are to make yourselves entirely at home.

[*To Mrs Lovett*]

The genius of the place has gone to get some photographs of your friend Petherick's bust of Edgar A. Poe, the eminent literary man.

[*Turning to* LUCAS, *who has found something interesting on the table*]

Both of you remember Mr. Lucas, I suppose.

VILLA

[*In a voice of friendly surprise*]

Why it's George!

[*She goes to him and gives him her hand, which he takes slowly, and holds a little longer than he means to*]

Why, Auntie, it's George!

[*To* Lucas]

You remember my aunt, don't you, George?

LUCAS

I remember Mrs. Lovett very well.

MRS. LOVETT
[*without warmth*]

Of course I remember Mr. Lucas.

[*To* Otto]

And now, Otto, you bad child

[*Holding up her finger*]

oh, yes! I have read your wicked books, and I know just
how bad you are

[*Laughing*]

—Villa and I are perishing to see the picture in its new
frame.

[*To* Villa]

Shall we wait for dear Weldon to come back? Artists are
so queer, you know, and

[*To* Otto, *with a smile*]

so very sensitive.

OTTO
[*Beaming*]

Very sensitive indeed. Have you read my last one—
Au Cinquième? It came out day before yesterday.

VILLA
[*Amused*]

I'm sorry, Otto, but we haven't even seen it.

OTTO

[*Briskly*]

In that case,

[*To* Mrs. Lovett]

you cannot possibly know how bad I am.—As for the frame,

[*Moving towards the picture*]

the frame is a beautiful piece of work. In point of fact, I don't quite see how you are going to get along without it.

[Mrs. Lovett *follows him and they stand together before the picture.* Lucas *and* Villa *remain near the table, she becoming very serious and he pretending, not very well, to take a humorous view of the situation*]

MRS. LOVETT

[*After a silence*]

Aren't you coming to see yourself, Villa?

VILLA

I'll watch you and Otto—and talk with George. I know just how the picture looks, and I haven't seen George for a thousand years.

[Mrs. Lovett *frowns a little and* Otto *smiles to himself significantly*]

MRS. LOVETT

[*Looking at the picture*]

Oh—dear!

[*She sighs and looks at* Otto, *who stands on his toes for a moment and then shakes his head*]

VILLA

[*Turning from* Lucas *to* Mrs. Lovett, *and laughing*]

What's the matter, Auntie?

MRS. LOVETT

[*With ample resignation*]

I don't know what to say about it.

[*She looks at* LUCAS, *who does not see her, and then looks at* OTTO]

You say something, Otto.   I simply don't know how.

OTTO

I would gladly be of assistance, my dear Madam, but I don't know how to say anything about it either.

[*Looking at* LUCAS]

But there's Lucas; he knows how to say something about it.

MRS. LOVETT

[*After a quick frown*]

Tell me the truth, Otto.

[*She sighs again*]

VILLA

·[*Turning and laughing*]

If you do, Otto, I'll tell Weldon everything you say.

OTTO

[*Looking from* VILLA *to* MRS. LOVETT, *with a grimace*]

You seem to know the truth already.   If you don't, I cannot tell a lie.

[*Very distinctly*]

In the last analysis, then, the thing is worse than—than office-hours.

VILLA

[*With determination*]

I'm going to say something now.   I'm going to ask Otto

to turn that picture to the wall until Weldon comes back.
I won't have it abused.

[*To* LUCAS, *with sorry laugh*]

The only trouble with that picture is that it isn't *me*.

LUCAS
[*Drily*]

Yes, that is one trouble with it.

[VILLA *looks at him strangely, and laughs again as before.* MRS.
    LOVETT *looks at her with mild disapproval.* OTTO *grins,
    and begins to sing the swan-song in Lohengrin with subdued
    satisfaction as he turns the easel. As* OTTO *comes back to
    the center of the stage, the bell rings, and all appear to be
    suddenly disturbed*]

MRS. LOVETT

Now who in the world is that? We don't want people.

LUCAS

You might find out, Otto.

OTTO

Aye, aye, sir.

[*Becoming more exuberant, he propels himself towards the door
    with a series of quasi-nautical hitches, trumpeting with his
    lips the opening chorus in "Pinafore."* LUCAS *watches him
    with a weary smile,* VILLA VANNEVAR *laughs, and* MRS.
    LOVETT *looks bewildered.* OTTO *opens the door and stands
    back, in whimsical obeisance*]

OTTO

You may come in, for I know your name. Your name
is Van Zorn, and I've seen you before.

[Van Zorn Enters. He *is rather tall, well built, bronzed, and has powerful, penetrating eyes. His manner, though courteous and possibly a bit too dignified, is also a little heavy. He seems to be in constant fear of being taken too seriously; and yet he is a very serious person, inclined to a certain intangible melancholy that is easy to recognize but difficult to describe. His voice is rich, deep, and musical, his laugh is rare but pleasing, but his smile is frequent and engaging. There is at times something childlike in his acceptance of unusual situations and events, and there is something almost unreal in his easy persistence along lines that few men would ever think of pursuing. While he is for the most part self explanatory, there remains a fringe of mystery about him to the end*]

VAN ZORN

[*Taking* Otto's *hand and smiling*]

And I should remember *your* name. Your name is . . .

OTTO

[*Distinctly*]

Mink.

VAN ZORN

[*With another smile*]

Indeed? Then you must have two names.

OTTO

[*As the two move into the room*]

I have. The grand total is Otto Mink.

VAN ZORN

I remember now that Farnham called you Otto. I am very glad to see you again.

OTTO

[With expansion]

And now it devolves upon me to present a few of Farn-ham's friends. Here, for example, is Mrs. Lovett.

[She smiles at Otto, and receives Van Zorn with unqualified approval]

And here is Miss Villa Vannevar. She's another friend of Farnham's, and you've met her before.

[VILLA gives VAN ZORN her hand, and he looks at her, in spite of his efforts, as if he were fascinated. The two appear to be very serious, until OTTO presents LUCAS, when she laughs— but with no great amount of spirit]

And here is Mr. Lucas. Sometimes we call him Phœbus— on account of his sunny disposition.

[VAN ZORN shakes hands with LUCAS with great cordiality and looks at him as long as he looked at VILLA VANNEVAR, but with an entirely different expression. There is a kindness and a certain satisfaction in his eyes that surprises LUCAS and embarrasses him]

That object over there is a portrait of Miss Vannevar, but we are not to see it again until Farnham comes back. You won't like Farnham any better after you see it.

VAN ZORN

[Amused]

That doesn't sound altogether complimentary to Farnham.

OTTO

[Cheerfully]

It isn't.

VAN ZORN

Perhaps I don't quite understand you.

OTTO

You will.

VAN ZORN

[*With a look of amused inquiry at* LUCAS]

You surprise me. I have come to think of Farnham as one of the best of living painters.

OTTO

[*With his hands in his trousers' pockets*]

He is. That's partly what ails him.

MRS. LOVETT

Why, Otto,—you ridiculous child!

OTTO

If you don't believe me, ask Phœbus—I mean Lucas.

VAN ZORN

[*To* VILLA, *smiling*]

I think I'll wait and ask Farnham himself.

VILLA

[*Laughing*]

He may bite you.

VAN ZORN

I know Farnham's bite. It isn't very dangerous.

VILLA

He thinks it is.

VAN ZORN

[*Moving nearer to her, as if drawn*]

How soon do you expect him back?

VILLA

[*Suddenly serious*]

At any moment.

[Lucas *begins a silent investigation of the studio, while* Mrs. Lovett *and* Otto *talk together,* Mrs. Lovett *apparently amused and perhaps a little scandalized by his childlike narrations. She looks frequently and almost eagerly at* Van Zorn *and* Villa, *who stand near the table. They seem to be laboring under a mysterious constraint, which* Villa *tries to put off with an assumed light humor*]

VAN ZORN

[*Smiling*]

You talk as if you thought me a doubtful character. I trust that Farnham hasn't given me one.

VILLA

[*Nervously*]

Weldon has praised you so much that we are all a little afraid of you.

VAN ZORN

I shall have to stop that.

[*Pause*]

Do you remember the day when you and Mr.—

[*Glancing at* Otto]

Mr. Mink—went over my boat with Farnham and me?

VILLA

Of course I do. That was the day before you sailed away to the other side of the world.

VAN ZORN
[*Earnestly*]

Thank you for remembering that day.

VILLA
[*Still nervous*]

I remember the day—and I remember that you frightened me somehow.
[*Laughing*]
You made me think of Captain Kidd and the Flying Dutchman—both together.

VAN ZORN
[*Smiling*]

I don't know about Captain Kidd, but I suppose I *am* a sort of Dutchman.

VILLA
[*With a little shiver*]

Not the Flying Dutchman—I hope?

VAN ZORN
[*With a quaint seriousness*]

No—not exactly. As a matter of fact, I have undertaken to be a doctor.

VILLA
[*Bewildered*]

Medicine, Philosophy or Divinity?

VAN ZORN
[*With a melancholy laugh.*]

All three, in a measure—and I shall be my own patient.

[*Quite seriously*]

I must have a place in the scheme of existence, and I have had a presentiment that I am soon to find it.

VILLA

[*Drawing back a little and laughing*]

You? . . . A place in the scheme of existence? . . . I'm beginning to be positively creepy. I thought you had everything.

VAN ZORN

[*Shaking his head*]

Then you are greatly mistaken. I have nothing—yet.

VILLA

[*Impulsively*]

What a very unfortunate person! I beg your pardon a thousand times, but you make me laugh.

VAN ZORN

You needn't be apologetic, and you needn't laugh.

VILLA

[*Bewildered*]

What—are you going to do—first?

VAN ZORN

[*Smiling faintly*]

I have thought of several plans to make my existence worth while, but I am not yet sure of any of them.

VILLA

[With a sigh and a laugh]

Well, I don't know what you expect me to say. You don't speak a language that a poor girl can understand.

[She looks over her shoulder and meets the eyes of LUCAS, *who by this time has made a circuit of the studio and taken a casual inventory of its contents. She looks at him, smiling, and then at* VAN ZORN, *who is looking at* LUCAS *with a slight frown that is both friendly and inquiring]*

VILLA

I wonder if George—Mr. Lucas—could be of any service to you. He isn't a doctor, but he knows almost everything.

VAN ZORN

[Pleasantly, after a slow nod at LUCAS]

Does he know himself?

LUCAS

[With a shrug]

I regret to say that he does.

VAN ZORN

[To LUCAS, *distinctly]*

Then Miss Vannevar is right. The man who knows himself does know almost everything.

[There has been a brief pause in OTTO'S *animated conversation with* MRS. LOVETT, *and now* OTTO *looks keenly at* VILLA, VAN ZORN, *and* LUCAS]

VILLA

[*Laughing at* OTTO]

The man who knows himself must be inspired.

[*To* VAN ZORN]

Otto couldn't keep from being inspired if he tried. Otto is a poet.

OTTO

[*Grinning*]

Do I look like one?

VILLA

You look like a rose of Sharon, Otto.

[*Glancing towards the door*]

I thought I heard something.

OTTO

[*Holding up his finger*]

Hist! There it is again!

[*Going to the door mysteriously*]

It's the Thing itself.

[FARNHAM *is heard in the vestibule, singing carelessly to himself the air of the Conspirators from "La Fille de Madame Angot."* OTTO *opens the door with a flourish, and* FARNHAM *soon enters*]

OTTO

You are late, and the show is half over.

[*Putting his hands into his trousers' pockets*]

The next thing on the programme will be the eminent comedians, Van Zorn and Lucas, in "The Old Oaken Bucket." Song and dance.

MRS. LOVETT

[*With languid primness*]

Otto, you might take your hat and go home.

FARNHAM

[*Taking* MRS. LOVETT's *hand*]

No, don't send him home. He can't help it. The trouble is in his brain.

[HE *shakes hands with* VILLA *and smiles*]

But *you*

[*Shaking hands with* VAN ZORN *and looking at him with eager satisfaction*]

—you might have let a fellow know that you were coming.

[*looking around*]

I suppose there is no need of introductions.

OTTO

[*Beaming*]

None whatever. We are all happily acquainted.

FARNHAM

[*After giving* OTTO *a patronizing scrutiny*]

There are the photographs, Mrs. Lovett, and if you don't find them sufficiently bad, it won't be Petherick's fault. Poor Poe!

[*Nodding to* VAN ZORN]

He could tell you something about Destiny, if he were alive.

[*He nods at the envelope*]

MRS. LOVETT
[*Looking at one of the photographs*]

Poe was a wonderful creature.

FARNHAM

There are no records to prove that he ever denied it.
[*To* VILLA, *with his most confident smile*]
Have you seen the picture, and the frame?
[*He gazes at the easel, frowns for a moment, and then laughs drily*]
Who turned it to the wall?   Did you do that, Lucas?

VILLA
[*Quickly*]

Otto did it.   I told him to.

FARNHAM
[*Rather drily*]

That was very considerate of you.
[HE *moves the easel back to its former position*]
Well, there it is.
[*Confidently*]
And now you may all do your worst.   Otto and Lucas
needn't say anything, for I know what they think already.

OTTO
[*Cheerfully*]

You may not.   We've never told you.

FARNHAM
[*With a short laugh*]

Well, if you haven't, you needn't.
[VAN ZORN *stands before the picture and studies it ominously*]

FARNHAM

Well, which is it—life, or death?

VAN ZORN

[*With annihilating deliberation*]

I should say that it was neither. I am not satisfied with it.

FARNHAM

[*With a dry laugh*]

Were you ever entirely satisfied with anything?

VAN ZORN

[*Gently*]

We are not here on earth to be entirely satisfied, are we?

FARNHAM

Oh, I don't know about that.

VAN ZORN

I hope most sincerely that you are not satisfied with this picture.

FARNHAM

I thought it had a kind of merit.

VAN ZORN

[*Frowning*]

It has. It's a work of genius, if you like.

OTTO

[*Promptly*]

That's what *I* said.

FARNHAM
[*Patiently*]

I know it Otto—And now I should like to hear what Mrs Lovett has to say.

MRS. LOVETT

But, dear Weldon, you can't possibly care what I think—a poor old thing like me.

[*Looking through her glasses*]

Of course you have flattered the poor child almost to death.

FARNHAM
[*Genially*]

I don't see how you can say so.

VILLA

[*To* VAN ZORN *and* LUCAS]

Help! help!

MRS. LOVETT

But you are a wonderful creature, all the same, and I shall have to forgive you.   Two very intelligent men

[*Beaming on* OTTO]

have called you a genius, and surely that should be enough for one morning.

OTTO

Three, Mrs. Lovett, Phœbus—I mean George—called him one before you came in.

MRS. LOVETT

[*After a look at* LUCAS]

I am very glad to hear it.

OTTO

[*Briskly*]

I knew you would be.

[*Going to* LUCAS]

And now, Phœbus—I mean George—it's time for you and me to go out and have something to eat. I have a premonition that you and I are in a way to become superfluous.

MRS. LOVETT

[*With motherly tolerance*]

Otto, are you going to talk nonsense all the rest of your life?

OTTO

[*Spinning his hat on the end of his stick*]

If youth but knew.

VILLA

[*With animation*]

Why can't we all go out and lunch somewhere together? I've got some money.

MRS. LOVETT

You forget, my child, that we are to have luncheon with Mrs Dyce.

OTTO

Give my love to Mrs. Dyce, and to the Pomeranian twins. And now Phœbus and I are going over to the Brevoort House and have something with a squeezed lime in it. After that we shall have a morsel of bread, and Phœbus will tell me what he thinks of my new book—*Au Cinquième*, I call it.

[*To* VILLA]

You haven't seen it.　Are you going to be at home this afternoon?

VILLA

[*Laughing*]

Yes, Otto, —to *you*.

OTTO

All right.　I'll bring around a copy of *Au Cinquième*. [*cheerfully*] I wrote it with my heart's blood.

[*To* LUCAS, *briskly*]

Come along, Phœbus.

VILLA

[*Going to* LUCAS *and holding out her hand*]

Good-bye, George.

LUCAS

[*Taking her hand and speaking strangely*]

Good-bye.

VAN ZORN

[*Giving* LUCAS *his hand*]

I am very glad to have met you, Mr. Lucas—very glad indeed.

[HE *speaks with a peculiar earnestness that causes* MRS. LOVETT *and* FARNHAM *to look at each other.　But* LUCAS *appears to be abstracted and indifferent*]

OTTO

[*At the door, declaiming solemnly*]

"So now for a season we leave you, taking with us our various musical instruments.　Presently we shall return, bringing with us nothing but our accordeons." *Auf wiedersehen*.

[OTTO *and* LUCAS *go out.* MRS. LOVETT *and* FARNHAM *look after* OTTO *and laugh.* VAN ZORN *looks at* VILLA VANNEVAR, *who stands gazing at the floor. Her face is troubled and she bites her under lip as if to keep it under control*]

MRS. LOVETT
[*To* FARNHAM]

Otto should be ashamed of himself.

FARNHAM

He will be—sometime.

MRS. LOVETT

He is going to take that poor unfortunate Mr. Lucas over to the Brevoort House and give him liquor.

FARNHAM
[*With an unfeeling grin*]

I don't see any way out of it now. As for poor Mr. Lucas, this man

[*Looking at* VAN ZORN]

will tell you that he is in the hands of Destiny—gin-rickeys and all.

[*With a laugh*]

We can do nothing for him.

MRS. LOVETT
[*Rising with a sigh*]

It may be so, poor fellow. If he were not so thoroughly impossible, he would be rather interesting.

[VILLA *looks at her almost angrily*]

VAN ZORN

May I venture to ask, Mrs. Lovett, if you are final in your judgment?

MRS. LOVETT

[*With apologetic vivacity*]

Dear me, no! I don't judge anything—not even a fly.

VAN ZORN

[*Smiling, as if with effort*]

I am very glad, for I have begun to believe that Mr. Lucas and I may be of service to each other.

[VILLA *looks at him eagerly*]

MRS. LOVETT

[*Puzzled and not wholly pleased*]

I don't understand what you mean, and I'm not going to try.

VAN ZORN

I am not always sure that I understand myself.

VILLA

[*With a nervous laugh*]

I'm glad to know it, for I'm not either.

[*To* MRS. LOVETT]

Come along, Auntie, or Mrs. Dyce's little dogs will eat up all the luncheon.

[*Laughing*]

Pomeranian twins!

[*Giving her hand to* VAN ZORN]

Good bye . . . I'm glad you aren't the Flying Dutchman.

VAN ZORN
[*Holding her hand*]
Nothing half so distinguished, I assure you.

VILLA
[*Not wholly at ease*]
Or so unfortunate.

VAN ZORN
[*Letting her hand go, slowly*]
I am not so sure about that.

VILLA
Weldon thinks you are the greatest man in the world
[*To* FARNHAM, *laughing*]
—except himself.

MRS. LOVETT
[*Beaming*]
And the most wonderful creature.

VAN ZORN
[*Smiling*]
Weldon has made a mistake.

VILLA
You are too modest.

VAN ZORN
Do you think so?

VILLA
[*With the same constrained laugh*]
Perhaps I don't know you well enough to say.

VAN ZORN

We may come to know each other better in the future.

VILLA

I feel sure of that. I should like to know you better.

VAN ZORN
[*Smiling*]
You may be disappointed in me.

VILLA
[*As before*]
If I am, I'll tell you so.

MRS. LOVETT
[*Who has been watching the two with bewildered approval*]
She means that she will say, on all occasions, the first thing that comes into her silly little head.—But we must go now. Good-bye.

[THEY *shake hands.* VAN ZORN *and* VILLA VANNEVAR *look at each other with a smile of half-fascinated intensity. The two women go*]

FARNHAM
[*Coming from the door and touching* VAN ZORN *on the shoulder, laughing curiously*]
Well, Childe Harold, for a sedate and rather melancholy Ancient Mariner, you seem to be getting on.

VAN ZORN
[*Standing in thought*]
Yes, I am getting on in years.

FARNHAM

Oh, cheer up. We are only thirty two. "We are children still," and we "grope in the dark for what the day will bring."

[*Going to the table and reaching for the cigars*]

That's what we do: we "grope in the dark for what the day will bring" . . . Here—have a cigar.

VAN ZORN

[*Absently*]

No, thank you.

FARNHAM

[*Holding out the box*]

It's a Pedro.

VAN ZORN

No, thank you.

FARNHAM

[*Coaxingly*]

Colorado.

VAN ZORN

Not now.

FARNHAM

[*Taking a cigar and putting back the box*]

Well, is there anything that your serene excellency *would* like, that I can give you—this fine October morning? You'll have a drink, perhaps.

VAN ZORN

[*Shaking his head*]

No, Farnham. But I may—I may ask you for your advice.

FARNHAM

[*Lighting his cigar*]

And you couldn't possibly do better.   What seems to be weighing most heavily on your noble mind?

[*Pointing to a chair*]

Sit down.

[VAN ZORN *takes the large chair mechanically and remains for a time in silence.* FARNHAM *sits expectantly in a small chair not far from the table*]

VAN ZORN

[*Slowly*]

Farnham, I wish you would tell me something about this man Lucas. . . .   About his life, and his death, and his possibilities.

FARNHAM

[*Laughing*]

His death, did you say?

VAN ZORN

[*Simply*]

Yes.   He seems to have died.

FARNHAM

[*Carelessly*]

I don't know but you are right.   And if you refer to his possibilities in the way of drink, I can recommend him without qualifications.   There is nothing else in town that is quite like him.

VAN ZORN

I am not joking, I assure you.

FARNHAM

Neither am I. Old Hundred is no joke.

VAN ZORN

Then you might tell me something about him. Who is he? What is he? And why is he where he is?

FARNHAM

[*Laughing*]

Where *is* he?

VAN ZORN

He appears just now to be at what we might call the crossways. Whether he takes one way or the other, will depend upon events.

FARNHAM

[*With a short laugh*]

Why don't you say Destiny, and be done with it?

VAN ZORN

Very well—we'll call it Destiny. How old is Lucas?

FARNHAM

About twenty-nine. Abundantly old enough to know better.

VAN ZORN

[*With a smile*]

You might say that of *me*. It is possible that Lucas and I may have a great deal in common.

[*He taps the arms of his chair with his fingers and looks into the distance*]

FARNHAM

[*Laughing impatiently*]

I thought of that when I saw you together.

[*Crossing his legs*]

Well, you ask me to tell you about Lucas, and I find that
I haven't much to tell. I haven't known him very long,
when it comes to that; but from what I have gathered and
inferred, it would seem that his father was a good deal of a
metropolitan rounder—before the days of the Great White
Way. Whether that made any difference or not, I don't
know. All I can say for certain is that Lucas's father
didn't spend all his evenings holding his little one on his
knee, or teaching him the binomial theorem.

[*With a tired sigh*]

Little Georgie was undoubtedly neglected. But what of
it?

[*Looking at the bust*]

So was Shakespeare, I fancy.

VAN ZORN

[*Frowning*]

And Lucas's mother?

FARNHAM

She had the good fortune to die.   You needn't look at me
like that, for the old man was a bad egg.

VAN ZORN

[*Disappointed*]

Is that the best you can do for me?

FARNHAM

[*Impatiently*]

What more do you want? It's for Lucas to do the rest. He has ability enough to fit out a dozen ordinary men, but he can't use it—or he won't. He isn't peculiar to New York. You'll find him over all the world.

VAN ZORN

[*Thoughtfully*]

And Lucas has run down—like a watch.

FARNHAM

Yes, or rather like the Old Clock on the Stairs. And I'm afraid he's past winding up.

VAN ZORN

[*Tapping with his fingers*]

And what will be the outcome of all this?

FARNHAM

[*Weary of the subject*]

Oh, I don't know. I shouldn't wonder if I were to take up a newspaper some morning and read that one George Lucas had blown the top of his head off in one of our public parks—probably in Washington Square, not far from the statue of Garibaldi. That statue beats anything of Petherick's.

VAN ZORN

[*Slowly*]

I wonder if I have made a mistake. I don't often make mistakes in my judgment of men.

FARNHAM

That's interesting.　How about women?

VAN ZORN

We are not talking about women—

[*With emphasis*]

at present.

FARNHAM

[*Laughing*]

All right; excuse me.　But what if you *do* make mistakes?
You can charge them all up to Destiny, and go on about
your business.　The rest of us poor devils, who think we are
burdened with free will, have to pay for our mistakes—
with complex interest.

VAN ZORN

No matter about that.　But what if *I* were to run down—
after the manner of Lucas?

FARNHAM

But Lucas's case hasn't anything to do with yours.

VAN ZORN

How do you know?

FARNHAM

You couldn't let yourself run down.

VAN ZORN

How do you know?

FARNHAM

[*Getting up, with a laugh of protest*]

Because that isn't the way we do things nowadays—if
we have any sense. If you say "How do you know"
again, I'll . . .

VAN ZORN

Farnham, has it occurred to you that Lucas's problem
may not be half so simple as you have made it out to be?

FARNHAM

You can't expect me to tell you what I don't know.

VAN ZORN

[*Significantly*]

Or all that you do know—possibly.

[FARNHAM *says nothing, but smokes*]

In the light of what you say, I wonder that you should
trouble yourself to have this man Lucas around.

FARNHAM

More Destiny I suppose. We can't beat Destiny.

VAN ZORN

Certainly not. But Destiny can beat *us*, and it can make
us do better than we have done in the past.

FARNHAM

[*With a sharp look*]

So Lucas is going to have greatness thrust upon him,
is he?

[*Laughing*]

"Van Zorn and Lucas, the eminent comedians."

VAN ZORN

[*Laughing a little and looking at the bust*]

I wonder what Shakespeare would do if he were in my place.

FARNHAM

He might kill Polonius, or he might mix himself a drink. That would depend entirely upon Destiny.

VAN ZORN

[*Drily*]

Undoubtedly . . . and we might say more about Destiny . . . But whether or not we ought to say it . . .

FARNHAM

According to your convenient doctrine, I don't see that there is any "ought" or "ought not" about it—unless you think you ought to congratulate me on my engagement to Villa Vannevar. Do you?

VAN ZORN

[*Distinctly, after a pause*]

Most assuredly *not*.

[VAN ZORN *drums with his fingers on the arms of his chair and looks straight before him.* FARNHAM *watches him with a gathering hardness in his look and at length breaks the strained silence with a flat laugh, to which* VAN ZORN *pays no attention*]

FARNHAM

[*Uncomfortably*]

Is this a new kind of joke that you have brought with you from India? If it is, I don't seem to care much for it.

VAN ZORN

[*Looking at him*]

I wish, Farnham, that you would wait a little before you talk like that.

FARNHAM

[*With a short laugh*]

All right—I'll wait. There's nothing else for me to do. It's going to be Destiny anyhow, and I can't help myself.

VAN ZORN

[*After getting up and looking at the picture*]

Farnham, there is something wrong here.

[HE *moves slowly towards him*]

There is something in the air. I can feel it. I have felt it ever since I came in.

FARNHAM

[*Unpleasantly*]

Shall I open a window and let it out?

VAN ZORN

I think it would be quite sufficient if we were to—lift a curtain.

FARNHAM

[*Drily*]

On your past life?

VAN ZORN

On mine—and yours. Past, present, and future.

FARNHAM

You are sure that you are quite well?

VAN ZORN

[*Nods slowly*]

I am sure.

FARNHAM

[*With mock relief*]

That's good. Now a man in your condition ought to have a cheerful, not to say optimistic, outlook on life.

[HE *shrugs his shoulders and forces another laugh*]

VAN ZORN

[*Distinctly*]

I may not see life as it is, but I see it as I see it. And I am confident that I see one rather important aspect of it as it is going to be if you have your way. I mean, rather, if your vanity and your obstinacy have *their* way.

FARNHAM

[*With a sign of resignation*]

Go on.

[*Drily*]

You are the best thing we have had since Samson and the foxes. Well, with my Vanity and your Destiny working together, we ought to arrive somewhere, as I have no doubt we shall.

VAN ZORN

And where do you think we shall arrive?

FARNHAM

If you'll be good enough to raise that magic curtain of yours, we may find out.

VAN ZORN
[*Frowning*]

If I raise it—yes.

FARNHAM
[*Nervously*]

Then why the devil don't you?

[*Laughing as before*]

I can stand it—Destiny and all.

[*With assumed lightness*]

I am enjoying what you say, thus far; and I have no doubt

[*Sitting down*]

that I shall be interested in what may follow.

VAN ZORN
[*After watching* FARNHAM]

Then I may as well come to my subject. Do you know that I have been coming to it for a long time—for more than four years, in fact?

FARNHAM

I don't know what you are talking about, but go ahead, all the same.

VAN ZORN

I will. And I'll begin by asking you one or two direct questions. If they seem too direct, you must try to pardon me.

[*Pause*]

Farnham, does the approaching unhappiness of three people, who might as well be happy, commend itself to you as an attractive picture, or as a desirable state of affairs? Have you said to yourself that your Vanity and my Destiny, to use your own words, might as easily work together for joy and for good, as for misery and for evil?

FARNHAM

[*Squirming*]

What name does your doctor give to this?

VAN ZORN

Don't you think we are beyond that now?

FARNHAM

[*Nervously*]

Beyond recovery? I hope not.

VAN ZORN

Haven't I raised the curtain?

FARNHAM

[*Getting up*]

You have raised the devil. That's about what you have done.

[*With another dry laugh*]

What have you been doing since you went away?

VAN ZORN

[*Quietly*]

You give me a leverage when you ask that.

FARNHAM

[*Impulsively*]

Then for God's sake use it, and send this curtain of yours up a little higher.

[*With irony*]

If I can be of any assistance . . .

VAN ZORN

[*Distinctly*]

Farnham, my career, during the past four years, has consisted for the most part in *seeking* . . . seeking for guidance.

FARNHAM

[*With another laugh*]

You might have done worse. "He that seeketh" . . . You know about that fellow.

VAN ZORN

[*Slowly, but with finality*]

"Findeth."

FARNHAM

[*With strained humor*]

Good. Are you sure you won't have a cigar?

VAN ZORN

[*Solemnly*]

Do you remember what the text goes on to say of him that knocketh? I wonder what you think would be likely to happen if I were to—knock.

[FARNHAM *moves to the fireplace and stands gazing into the grate.* VAN ZORN *looks at him and waits for him to speak*]

FARNHAM

[*Slowly and incredulously*]

What are you driving at, anyhow? Are you in love with Villa Vannevar? . . . You have never told me about this.

VAN ZORN

You have not been exactly available.

FARNHAM

You might have come back before.

VAN ZORN

And I might have made a mistake in doing so. I waited for what seemed to be the appointed time, and then I came.

FARNHAM

And here you are.

[*With more spirit*]

Now I don't know much about the appointed time, as you call it, but I suppose I do know what you mean by knocking at doors.

[*He looks at the picture and scowls*]

May I ask

[*Unpleasantly*]

how many times you intend to knock? And when you intend to begin?

VAN ZORN

[*In a level, musical voice*]

My intention was to knock once, this afternoon, if it could be arranged.

FARNHAM

[*Incredulously*]

You and your boat must have made a record, if that's the way you feel.

[*As if led along reluctantly by the humor of the situation*] Well, I dare say it can be arranged—and I infer that you count on me to do the arranging.

VAN ZORN

I shall never knock under other conditions.

FARNHAM

[*As before*]

And what do you intend to do after you get in? Something in the Lochinvar line? Carry the young lady away on a horse—or in a limousine?

VAN ZORN

[*Seriously*]

If I were to be admitted, and if I were to satisfy myself that my convictions are correct, that three people are on their way to unhappiness and disaster. . . . What should I do then? What ought I to do then?

FARNHAM

You look at me as if you thought I was afraid of something. I wish you would tell me what *I* ought to be beginning to think of *you*.

VAN ZORN

[*Quietly*]

You should think of me at all times as the best friend you have in the world.

[FARNHAM *lights a match on the box that he has taken from the mantel and watches the flame until it burns down to his fingers. Then he puts his hands into his pockets and looks at* VAN ZORN *intently*]

FARNHAM

[*Distinctly*]

How long has this been going on? How long have you been planning to marry Villa Vannevar?

VAN ZORN

[*Distinctly*]

I said something about four years. But time, in your sense of the word, doesn't mean very much to me.

FARNHAM

[*Almost with a sneer*]

It may come to mean more—eventually

VAN ZORN

[*Nods slowly*]

That remains to be seen.

FARNHAM

[*As before*]

As you see it?

[VAN ZORN *nods again*]

My fatalistic friend, you may not care much to know what I have been doing during the past four or five years, but what I have been doing during the past four or five minutes may be of interest to you. If so, I have been asking myself why it is, in spite of my agreement, that I have been

taking the trouble to listen to you. You must be aware
that I would not have listened to the same talk from any
other man living.

VAN ZORN

[*With a strange innocence*]

What possible fear can you have, if you have no doubts—
or misgivings?

FARNHAM

[*Scowling*]

Fear? Doubts? Misgivings?—what the devil are you
driving at now?

VAN ZORN

[*As before*]

You might lead me to believe that you think me capable
of treachery.

FARNHAM

Treachery?

[*With a nasal laugh*]

By treachery, I suppose you mean

[*Letting his words out half-angrily, in detached phrases*]

the repeated visitations—of an irresistible personality—
on the unschooled emotions—of a young lady who is about
to do me the honor of becoming my wife. . . . Am I
about right?

VAN ZORN

[*Smiling*]

You speak now as if you thought me capable of almost
anything—beginning with murder.

FARNHAM

[*Trying to laugh*]

No, I don't think that. For I know now that even you
have your limitations.

VAN ZORN

[*With tightening lips*]

Yes; and I am limited, for the present, at any rate,
to one interview—subject to your consent and arrange-
ment. If by any chance you should choose to change
your mind . . .

FARNHAM

[*Half-angry*]

What do you mean by that? Why should I change my
mind? Just because you have elected to be plain crazy—
with your appointed time, and your—your Destiny—do
you think I'm going to be such an ass as to take you
seriously? I don't care much for this sort of thing, and
I don't mind telling you so; but if you insist upon making
a show of yourself, I don't know that I am bound by
courtesy to interfere, or by law to be responsible—under
the circumstances.

VAN ZORN

That will be first rate—especially under the circumstances. Now let me be sure that we both understand.
If I call to see Miss Vannevar this afternoon at four
o'clock, by special appointment,—or, if not then, at the
earliest opportunity . . .

FARNHAM

[*With an incredulous laugh*]

Oh, you'll get in. You needn't worry about that.

[*He smiles to himself and shakes his head, with a long sigh*]
Shall we go out now and have something to eat?

VAN ZORN
[*Smiling*]
Don't you think, Farnham, that we had better give each other a short leave of absence?

FARNHAM
[*Drily*]
As you say.
[*With a sorry laugh*]
As you see it.

VAN ZORN
Will you dine with me this evening?

FARNHAM
I'm sorry, but I can't. But I'll be here at ten, if that will do you any good.

VAN ZORN
[*Laughing a little*]
Then I shall see you at ten. And you will telephone me at my hotel—we'll say at three-thirty?

FARNHAM
[*With an easy snarl*]
Yes, I'll telephone.

VAN ZORN
The Knickerbocker.

FARNHAM

[*Wearily*]

I know it.

VAN ZORN

Then I'll say good-bye until—ten.

FARNHAM

[*More wearily*]

I understood what you said. You said ten.

[*After a pause* VAN ZORN *goes out.* FARNHAM *returns from the
vestibule with his hat and stick. After turning the picture
to the wall, he stands for a while near the window-seat, shakes
his head slowly, puts his hat on slowly, sits down, and smiles
incredulously to himself. He draws figures on the floor
with his stick as the curtain falls*]

CURTAIN

ACT II

ACT II

A diagonal view of a room in MRS. LOVETT'S *house. The right corner is revealed, with half of the right wall. In the corner is a small grand piano, and to the right is a window. To the left, half way down, is the entrance, a wide arched doorway with curtains. Well down in front, somewhat to the right, is a table, before which are two comfortable chairs that partly face each other. Against the wall, to the left and below the entrance, is a couch. There are several pictures on the walls, and over the piano is a portrait of* MRS. LOVETT'S *late husband, showing the beardless face of a man of fifty, melancholy and rather glowering. The room has the unmistakable appearance of a place where people live and make themselves at home.*

As the curtain rises, VILLA VANNEVAR *is at the piano, playing in a listless, abstracted manner the cantabile part of Chopin's Nocturne, Op. 37, No. 2.* MRS. LOVETT, *sitting in the chair at the right of the table, listens, frowns, stamps her foot, and finally speaks out with evident impatience.*

MRS. LOVETT
Villa Vannevar, do for heaven's sake keep still, or play something that has a little life in it. You play that thing as if you were crying through the ends of your fingers.

VILLA
[*Turning about and facing* MRS. LOVETT]
Would you have me always laughing, Auntie—like this?
[*She makes a ridiculous face and laughs*]

67

MRS. LOVETT

No, you silly child. But you needn't look forever as if life were nothing but one long funeral. I don't like funerals.

VILLA

[*With a shrug*]

I don't know about that. It seems to me sometimes that funerals are better than weddings. When we go to funerals, we know what has happened; but when we go to weddings, we don't even pretend to know what is *going* to happen.

[*Looking at her foot*]

I think I like funerals best.

MRS. LOVETT

You crazy child, you are positively wicked.

VILLA

Oh no, I'm not, Auntie. I'm good.

[*Getting up with a sigh*]

I'm good enough to be a fool.

MRS. LOVETT

[*As if scared*]

Villa Vannevar!

VILLA

[*Laughing*]

Yes, Auntie, that's what's the matter with me.

[*Wearily*]

Otto Mink and George Lucas believe already that I *am* one.

MRS. LOVETT

Child! Do you know what you are saying?

VILLA

[*Moving about with her hands behind her*]

I know perfectly well what I'm saying. They think I'm a fool for marrying Weldon Farnham—when he doesn't more than half want me.

MRS. LOVETT

[*Significantly, after a pause*]

You haven't married him yet.

VILLA

[*Trying to laugh*]

No, I have not.

[*Pause*]

I wonder if the other man—Mr. What-you-call-him—thinks I'm a fool.

MRS. LOVETT

[*With excited sarcasm*]

Don't you know what *he* thinks?

VILLA

How should I know what he thinks? I don't even know that he thinks at all.

[*With a pleasant nervousness*]

Do *you* know what he thinks?

MRS. LOVETT

I know that he considers you a very charming person, for one thing.

VILLA

[*Laughing*]

How nice of him! He didn't tell me so.

MRS. LOVETT

He may not have told *you*, but he did tell *me*. I am too old to be deceived.

VILLA

[*Laughing*]

Then you must be the oldest woman in the world.

MRS. LOVETT

[*With decayed archness*]

Possibly I am. In any case, I am old enough to see that he considers you not only very charming, but exceedingly impertinent.

VILLA

Then he must be a beast.

[*She laughs*]

MRS. LOVETT

He isn't a beast. He's a wonderful creature. And I am surprised out of my senses that he should be coming here to see you again this afternoon.

VILLA

[*Laughing*]

If you don't go away with your wonderful creatures, I shall throw things out of the window and shriek. For Mr. Van Zorn isn't a wonderful creature in the least. He's just a big overgrown man with a heap of money that he doesn't know what to do with, and he's coming to get you and carry you off in a taxicab.

[SHE *sits at* MRS. LOVETT'S *feet and looks up into her face*] And I'll never see my Auntie any more. And then I suppose there'll be nothing left for me to do but to go melancholy mad. I shall prowl around all by myself like a shut-up cat, and I'll sit down in all sorts of corners and cry like anything.

MRS. LOVETT

[*Pleased*]

So you have found his name at last, have you?

VILLA

I like his name. It sounds like a bassoon. But I don't like his eyes as well as I do the other man's.

MRS. LOVETT

[*Disturbed*]

Do you mean Weldon Farnham's?

VILLA

[*Calmly*]

No, I was thinking for the moment of George Lucas's eyes. Mr. What's-his-name's are too much like blue search-lights.

MRS. LOVETT

You needn't call him Mr. What's-his-name—and you needn't mention George Lucas. I am sorry that he has come to be what he is, but I don't care to have his name mentioned in my house.

VILLA

But you used to like him once, Auntie,—and this wonderful creature of yours liked him at first sight. As a matter of fact, he likes him better than he likes any of the rest of us.

MRS. LOVETT

Don't talk such nonsense.

VILLA

I'm not talking nonsense.

[*Laughing*]

Anyhow, Auntie, your wonderful creature has taken a wonderful fancy to George—I beg your pardon—and I don't know how you are going to change the course of events, even if you tell me that I have a head like an Edam cheese—which I haven't, in the least. My head makes Otto think of a very nice horse. He said so.

MRS. LOVETT

Otto may have said so because you act so much like a donkey.

VILLA

I don't act in any respect like a donkey, and I don't think you ought to say such things. For I am an extremely well-behaved young lady—except at times.

[*Pause*]

If you look at me like that much longer, Auntie, I'll say bow-bow; and then I'll put both my paws on your shoulders, and then I'll bite you.

[*She snaps her teeth and laughs*]

MRS. LOVETT

[*Reluctantly*]

My dear Villa, why did you bring up George Lucas's name again?

VILLA

[*With a kind of triumph*]

Why do *you* bring it up again, Auntie?

[*Pause*]

At any rate, he never injured anybody.

MRS. LOVETT

[*Sharply*]

But he disappointed everybody—and that's as bad as injuring them. I'm not sure that it isn't worse.

VILLA

But something may have happened.

MRS. LOVETT

Something always happens. What would be the use of living if things didn't happen?

VILLA

[*Slowly*]

I know. But if they happen at the wrong time, and under the wrong conditions . . .

MRS. LOVETT

[*With a sniff*]

Well, what do you mean? Do you mean that when a boy with more than ordinary brains chooses to make an utter fool of himself, and continues to do so until he grows up and everybody loses all patience with him . . .

[*She stops and looks angrily at her fingers*]

VILLA

[*Getting up and speaking thoughtfully*]

No, I don't mean just that . . . George's father must have been a very strange man.

MRS. LOVETT

[*Rapidly*]

It doesn't make any difference what you mean. Besides

[*Slowly, with significant vagueness*]

if you consider yourself engaged to Weldon Farnham, you ought not to think of other men at all. And you are not supposed to know anything about men like George Lucas's father.

VILLA

[*Laughing*]

You did that very badly, Auntie.

[*With mock-deliberation*]

And so you want this new man with the queer name—this wonderful creature—all to yourself!

[*Going behind* MRS. LOVETT *and putting her hands on her cheeks*]

And you're a dear, and you're a pig, and you want him all to yourself, and it's nearly time for him to come.

MRS. LOVETT

[*Shaking her head free and looking over her shoulder*]

Do you know that you grow sillier and sillier every day of your life?

VILLA

[*Drawing* MRS. LOVETT *back and looking down into her eyes*]

Well, would you have me stay forever and ever the same? . . . If you will roll your eyes back just a little farther, Auntie, I shall see myself in them—as I did when I was a little girl.

[*Pause*]

THE MAID

[*In the doorway*]

There is a gentleman to see Miss Villa. He gave me this card.

VILLA

[*Taking the card and examining it*]

But there's nothing on it.

[*She gives the card to* MRS. LOVETT *and laughs nervously*]

MRS. LOVETT

Dear me! I hope he isn't going to be eccentric.

VILLA

He may be an anarchist or something.

[*Shrugs and laughs*]

Go downstairs, Jenny, and find out the creature's name, and what he wants. If he asks for fish, give him a serpent.

MRS. LOVETT

[*Reprovingly*]

Villa!

MAID

His name is Mr. Lucas.

MRS. LOVETT

Then why didn't you say so?

VILLA

Tell him to come upstairs, Jenny.

[*The* MAID *goes out*]

MRS. LOVETT

[*Bewildered*]

What in the world does this mean? And what in the world do *you* mean by asking him to come upstairs?

VILLA

Heaven only knows, Auntie. I don't seem to know what anything means today.

[MRS. LOVETT *sits and frowns, and looks at her hands.* VILLA VANNEVAR *goes to the window and stands with her hands behind her back. Presently* MRS. LOVETT *turns and gazes at her, evidently much disturbed, and remains gazing at her until* LUCAS *enters.* HE *is pale, and his manner shows a constraint that he cannot wholly conceal. His clothes have been through some process of hasty renovation since his appearance in Act I*]

LUCAS

[*With a certain huskiness*]

I hope, Mrs. Lovett, that you will pardon this—I'll say this last intrusion on my part.

[VILLA *comes to him and takes his hand cordially, looking at him as if disturbed and anxious*]

MRS. LOVETT

[*Without warmth*]

Are you leaving New York, Mr. Lucas?

LUCAS

[*With assumed lightness*]

Yes; and it might have been better for me if I had gone long before this.

MRS. LOVETT

Indeed?

LUCAS

[*With impulsive directness*]

I came in the hope of seeing Miss Villa for a few moments before going away.

MRS. LOVETT

[*Rising slowly*]

Oh, I understand.

[*Reluctantly*]

In that case, I will leave you two to yourselves.

[LUCAS *and* VILLA *look at each other as she goes out. The faces of both are very serious and in hers there seems to be an expression of fear*]

VILLA

[*After a pause*]

Why did you send me a blank card?

LUCAS

[*With a thin laugh*]

Oh, I don't know. Because I drew it, I suppose. It wasn't a very brilliant performance on my part.

VILLA

[*With feeling*]

I don't think it was at all brilliant—or at all kind. You ought not to do such things, or say such things—to me.

LUCAS

[*With weak humor*]

I knew it wasn't brilliant as soon as I had done it.

[*At a venture*]

Your aunt was very good to leave us here together.

VILLA

Auntie is always good—

[*Hesitating*]

or means to be.

LUCAS

[*With a vague smile*]

I am glad to know that, for I should be sorry to leave you with an aunt who was not good. But I came only to say good-bye,—not to talk of family history, or of old times.

VILLA

Would any harm come of it if we did talk of old times?

[*She sits down on the chair at the right of the table*]

Please sit down.

LUCAS

No harm, I suppose, and not much good.

[*With a forced smile*]

No great good seems to have come of anything that I have done.

VILLA

[*Frowning anxiously*]

But I don't know what you have done.

[*Trying to laugh*]

You speak as mysteriously as Mr.—Mr. Van Zorn did this morning when he talked about his business.

LUCAS

[*Sitting down*]

Yes, Van Zorn and I have a great deal in common.

[*He speaks and smiles with mild bitterness*]

VILLA

[*Quickly*]

You may have. I couldn't keep from seeing that he took a great interest in you this morning.

LUCAS

[*As if tired, but still interested*]

If you could see that, you ought to be able to see almost anything. You ought even to be able to see what I have done.

VILLA

[*Angry with herself*]

But I didn't mean to say that. You know I didn't.

LUCAS

You might as well have meant to say it, for you must see that I have done nothing. Even Van Zorn took the trouble—did me the honor, if you insist—to see as much as that.

VILLA

[Lamely]

He saw that you were not—well, not quite satisfied. Isn't that what you mean?

LUCAS

Do you know anyone who is quite satisfied?

[Pause]

I know two or three who seem to be, but they are in asylums.

VILLA

[With a forced laugh and a shiver]

Oh! So that's where they are. I thought there must be something wrong.

LUCAS

[Standing up and speaking earnestly]

You are quite right. There *is* something wrong. We see it in the streets, we live it in our lives, we feel it in our hearts. And there you have my reason for coming to say good-bye to you.

VILLA

[Frightened]

You mustn't speak like that—as if we were never to see you again.

LUCAS

[As before]

And there you have my reason for wanting to go away into—what shall I call it?—into another kind of life, and to make a new beginning. It seems to be absolutely necessary, for many reasons, that I should make a new beginning. Yes, I want to get away from all this dust and deceit and disillusion; I want to get away from all this noise and poison; I want a place where I can be quiet for a while, away from streets and faces; I want a place where there are no roofs between me and the sky; I want a place where the sun shines down on a fellow, and where the stars are. . . . Oh yes, I know well enough what I want, and I know that I've waited too long. I might as well have gone away years ago . . .

VILLA

[*Looking down*]

Yes, it might perhaps have been as well.

LUCAS

It would have been better—far better.

VILLA

[*Looking up and hesitating*]

Won't you tell me where you are going?

LUCAS

[*After a pause*]

I am going—west.

VILLA

You are not very confidential.

LUCAS

I would be more so if I could.

VILLA

Mightn't it be better if you were to go in the other direction—towards the sunrise? . . . Was that a silly thing for me to say?

LUCAS

It will come to the same thing, for I shall follow the sun.
[*Trying to laugh*]
Some people do that all their lives—in order to keep warm.

VILLA

[*Also trying to laugh*]
Is that why you are going away? But you told me why you were going. I forgot.

LUCAS

I don't want you to forget that. What I want you to forget are some things that happened a long time ago.

VILLA

[*As before*]
Do be careful. You speak as if I were a hundred years old.

LUCAS

[*With strange earnestness*]
I'll be very careful, or at least I'll try to be. And will you be good enough to pardon me for not knowing at one time as much as I know now?—which God knows is little enough. I thought I knew myself then, but I've seen since that I was wrong. It was you who knew me. Yes, you knew me, then, and you know me still. And I am glad for that.

VILLA

[*Doubtfully*]

You don't speak as if you were glad . . . And I wonder if it is really worth while for us to be so serious over a matter that is—past—and—

LUCAS

Forgotten?

VILLA

[*Slowly*]

No, there is nothing that I wish to forget. We all make mistakes, don't we? How can we help ourselves?

[*She smiles sorrowfully*]

LUCAS

We were younger then than we are now.

VILLA

[*Forcing another laugh*]

I don't know what I shall do if you keep on telling me how old I am. Do you know that I pulled three gray hairs out of my poor scalp this morning?

[*He looks at her solemnly, and her face becomes suddenly serious*]

How long do you intend to stay in—the west?

[*Her question is obviously a makeshift to break the silence*]

LUCAS

There seems to be no answer to that question—for the present.

VILLA

But you are coming back sometime?

LUCAS

Who can tell? I may become so deeply attached to the region where I am going that I shall not wish to come back. Besides one has to consider the wisdom of his ways in this life—or he *should* consider them.

[*He speaks with a rather disastrous attempt at lightness that serves only to make* VILLA *more dissatisfied and unhappy than before*]

VILLA

[*Troubled*]

I don't understand what you mean.

LUCAS

[*With an effort*]

I don't mean very much.

[*Smiling faintly*]

But I came to say good-bye before going away—not to talk about wisdom.

VILLA

[*Looking at him as she rises*]

It was good of you to come.

LUCAS

[*Drearily*]

It was magnanimous of me.

[*With deep feeling*]

I wonder if you know how good you have been to me today?

VILLA

[*Trying again to laugh*]

My aunt has just been telling me that I am wicked.

LUCAS

[*After looking about the room*]

Well, good-bye.

[*He holds out his hand*]

VILLA

[*Holding his hand and speaking as if unwillingly*]

Good-bye . . . and I wish you every kind of good
fortune.

[*Pause*]

And I shall remember you—always—if you care.

LUCAS

[*With difficulty*]

Always? . . . Thank you . . . Good-bye . . .

[*As they stand looking into each other's eyes, the* MAID *appears
in the doorway and announces* "MR. VAN ZORN"]

VILLA

[*Dropping* LUCAS's *hand*]

Very well, Jenny. Tell him to come upstairs.

[*The* MAID *disappears,* VILLA *and* LUCAS *continue to look at
each other, and both appear now to be embarrassed. She
speaks again, after a pause*]

Please don't go—quite yet.

LUCAS

Why should I stay longer?

VILLA

[*Trying to laugh*]

I suppose I ought to keep him waiting, but I won't.

[*Seriously*]

For you are going away, and I feel sure that he would like to see you before you go . . . Isn't it odd that you two should be here together this afternoon?

LUCAS

[*Drily*]

It may be odd.

VILLA

[*Nervously*]

Or it may be fate.   Anyhow, I shan't let you go until you see him.

LUCAS

[*With tightened lips*]

Apparently not, unless I run.

VILLA

You aren't angry with me, are you?

LUCAS

I'm never angry, except with myself.

[*There is another pause, and* VAN ZORN *enters.   He looks at* VILLA VANNEVAR *and at* LUCAS, *but shows no surprise. He smiles pleasantly and shakes hands with* VILLA]

VAN ZORN

Ah!   I'm very glad to see you again.

[*Shaking hands with* LUCAS]

And I'm very glad to see Mr. Lucas again.

VILLA

[*Drawing her towards the door*]

Of course you will. What else can you do when two conspirators drive you out of your own room?

VAN ZORN

[*Pleased*]

Thank you. And when we have conspired sufficiently, I will play on the piano. Then you may come back.

[*The two women go out,* VILLA VANNEVAR *singing "Quand on Conspire" and laughing at the same time*]

VAN ZORN

[*Still smiling*]

Do you object to being corralled in this unconventional manner, Mr. Lucas?

LUCAS

[*Puzzled*]

I am entirely at your service.

VAN ZORN

[*In a very friendly voice*]

Well, to begin, it may possibly make you feel better to know that your friends have been talking about you behind your back.

[*He sits down on the piano stool, with his back to the keyboard*]

I refer to Farnham and myself.

[LUCAS *looks more puzzled*]

I'll be quite honest with you and tell you that I began it; and I may as well come to the point at once and tell you that I shall probably need you in my business,—assuming, you understand, that you are available. I have had three or four schemes in my head for some time, and I'm sure that you will find at least one of them congenial. Are you interested?

LUCAS

[*Taking an ivory paper cutter from the table*]

Yes, I am interested, but I don't want you to make a mistake.

VAN ZORN

[*Smiling*]

I shall make mistakes, whether you want me to or not. And as for what Farnham said—to go back for a little . . .

LUCAS

[*Drily*]

Let us go back, by all means. What Farnham said about me ought to make rather good copy.

[*Curiously*]

What sort of stuff has he been telling you?

VAN ZORN

He didn't tell me much.   In fact, far less than I hoped for.

[*Laughing a little*]

So you needn't worry about Farnham.

LUCAS

[*Looking at something on the wall and breaking the ivory paper cutter in his abstraction*]

I wasn't worrying about Farnham.

[*Fitting the pieces together*]

I was wondering about *you*.

[*Pause*]

Do you know what you are doing? . . . Do you know that you are taking me seriously?

VAN ZORN

[*With a friendly smile*]

If I were not taking you seriously, I should hardly have resorted, in a strange house, to this method of getting hold of you.

[*Half laughing*]

Don't you care to be taken seriously? Or do you prefer to be taken as a joke?

LUCAS

[*Hesitating*]

Why do you ask me if I care?

VAN ZORN

[*Pleasantly*]

Partly for the sake of saying something, and partly because I should like to know.

LUCAS

[*With tightened lips*]

Why don't you ask me the other question—and have it off your mind?

VAN ZORN

[*Indulgently*]

At your own suggestion, I will. I will ask if you care

enough to begin the game all over again, and let the past sink.

LUCAS

[*Cynically*]

The past ought to be pretty well drowned by this time.

VAN ZORN

[*Kindly, but very distinctly*]

On the contrary, I have been led to infer that you have put yourself to a great deal of trouble and expense to keep it floating, so to speak. As a rule, I don't mean to meddle with other people's affairs, but in your case . . .

[*With a laugh*]

I'm sure you understand me. You have a head of your own.

LUCAS

[*Nodding it slowly*]

Yes; and only one.

VAN ZORN

Do you think it worth saving?

LUCAS

[*Embarrassed*]

If you insist, I—well, I suppose I do. It's a fairly good head, in some respects. But why should we talk about it now?

[*He looks about him uneasily*]

VAN ZORN

[*Standing up and gazing at* LUCAS]

Because you told me you were going away. Now I will

be as frank as possible with you and tell you that I didn't
like your way of saying it, or your way of looking when you
said it.

LUCAS
[Wetting his lips]
You are not very clear.

VAN ZORN
[Seriously]
I am as clear as I can be, without having more specific
information.
[More seriously]
I knew another fellow once who—went away; and you
made me think of him.

LUCAS
[Drily]
How far did he go?

VAN ZORN
[Firmly]
How far did you intend to go?

LUCAS
[Nervously]
You seem to have it settled that I am not going.

VAN ZORN
[Smiling again]
You are not going if I can keep you in New York.

LUCAS

[*Throwing the broken paper cutter down on the table and putting his hands in his pockets*]

I thought I was going.

VAN ZORN

[*Frowning as he watches him*]

You speak as if you had made some final preparations. Sometimes they are very final indeed—preparations.

[*Pause*]

Will you give me an answer to my question if I ask you just what preparations you have made?

LUCAS

[*Slowly*]

Yes, and I will give you more than that.

VAN ZORN

[*Relieved*]

Good. But I'm not going to be satisfied even then. I am going to ask you, in addition, to dine with me this evening at the Knickerbocker, and I am going

[*He returns to the piano stool*]

to ask you to take a small advance.

[*Taking a check book and a pen from his pocket*]

If you don't happen to need this

[*He writes as he speaks*]

you needn't use it, but I want you to take it, all the same.

[*Handing him the check*]

Will you?

LUCAS

[*Slowly*]

Yes, I will take it.   And I will see you at—seven o'clock?

VAN ZORN

Thank you.

[*He toys with his pen as if he were waiting*]

LUCAS

And you may do whatever you like with this.

[*He takes a small vial from his waistcoat and gives it to* VAN ZORN, *who takes it slowly*]

VAN ZORN

[*Looking at the vial and scowling*]

Cyanide of potassium?

[*He smiles grimly and shakes his head as he looks up*]

That isn't what you need.

[*He looks again at the vial*]

K C N . . . do you know what that makes me think of?

[*He looks up again and laughs drily*]

LUCAS

[*Uncomfortably*]

Yes, I suppose I know.

VAN ZORN

[*Putting the vial in his pocket*]

No, I don't believe you do.

[*Smiling*]

It makes me think of Sir Joseph Porter, K. C. B.—in

Pinafore. The last letter is different, however. How does that thing go?

LUCAS

[*With sardonic distinctness*]

"When I was a lad, I served a term." You may not believe it, but I did.

VAN ZORN

Yes, I believe it. But I was thinking of the tune.

[*He turns on the stool and begins to drum with his right forefinger on the piano*]

Is that the way it goes?

LUCAS

[*With grateful impatience to get away*]

Yes—and this is the way I go.

[*Grasping* VAN ZORN'S *hand quickly*]

You will say something.

[*As if he had made a discovery*]

and *I* will say something.

[*Trying to hide his emotion in his voice*]

I'll make some sort of explanation.

[LUCAS *disappears quickly into the hall and* VAN ZORN *begins to drum "When I was a lad" once more on the piano.* VILLA VANNEVAR *appears in the doorway and watches him unseen. Finally she laughs and begins to clap her hands*]

VAN ZORN

[*Getting up*]

Mr. Lucas has gone.

[*Distinctly*]

But not so far as he thought he was going.

VILLA

[*Looking about*]

Did he go through the roof?

VAN ZORN

[*Smiling*]

No, he went by the way of the stairs—and rather suddenly.

VILLA

[*Puzzled*]

Did he leave any word behind him?

VAN ZORN

Well, yes. He told me to say something.

VILLA

What did he tell you to say?

VAN ZORN

[*Smiling*]

That was all—something.

VILLA

Please don't laugh at me.

VAN ZORN

Should I be likely to do that? Especially on so slight an acquaintance?

[*He laughs a little as he speaks, but* VILLA *remains serious*]

VILLA

[*Slowly*]

It doesn't seem to be slight—somehow.

VAN ZORN

[*With a touch of mystery*]

Perhaps it isn't, really. We mortals know very little of ourselves, and far less of each other. As a consequence, we make mistakes.

VILLA

[*Still puzzled*]

Do *you* make mistakes?

VAN ZORN

Frequently.

VILLA

[*With a nervous laugh*]

I'm so glad.

VAN ZORN

Do you know that many of us waste large fractions of our short lives in being sorry for our mistakes—and oftentimes when we should be glad for them?

VILLA

[*Puzzled*]

You said that as if you meant something.

VAN ZORN

[*Smiling*]

It is possible that I did mean something.

VILLA

Now you are laughing at me again.

VAN ZORN
[*Easily*]

Why should I laugh at you when I know that you are not happy?

VILLA
[*Puzzled*]

Do I look as if I were not happy?

VAN ZORN

Something has troubled you for a long time.

VILLA

Why do you say that?

VAN ZORN

If I had not known it, I should not have come to this house.

VILLA
[*Trying to laugh again*]

Did I look so utterly miserable this morning that you took pity on me? Was it the picture? Or did you think I took too much trouble to see that Weldon laughed at Mr. Lucas?

VAN ZORN
[*Frowning strangely*]

No, it was not that.

VILLA

You seem to know something about him.

VAN ZORN

About Lucas?

VILLA

Yes. You have kept him from going away. I am sure that he wished to go.

VAN ZORN

And I am sure that he intended to go. But I ventured to put the matter in a different light, and he has agreed to give New York another chance. New York, as I told him, is not in all respects the worst place in the world.

VILLA

[Laughing as before]

Weldon thinks it is. But I forgot to offer you a chair.

[Takes the chair at the left of the table]

I don't wonder that Auntie calls me all sorts of things.

VAN ZORN

Thank you.

[He puts his hands on the back of the chair at the left and looks at her as if waiting for her to say more]

VILLA

[Looking up at him]

Yes, he thinks New York is the very worst. And that, I suppose, is one of the reasons why we are going to Damascus.

[She laughs again, nervously]

VAN ZORN

[Slowly]

Damascus? . . . Why Damascus?

VILLA

Heaven only knows. And I am stupid enough to like New York. I like even the ferry whistles.

VAN ZORN

Should you care to stay here forever?

VILLA

No, I don't say that. I want to go to Egypt sometime and see the Sphynx. There are no sphynxes in New York.

VAN ZORN
[*Smiling*]

Are you sure of that?
[*She laughs*]
There are no ferry whistles in Damascus.

VILLA

Why do you object to my going?

VAN ZORN

Why should I?

VILLA

Why do you object to George Lucas's going—west?

VAN ZORN

Because I have taken a particular interest in him.

VILLA
[*Quickly*]

I'm glad of that.

[*With a slight constraint*]

For I have known him all my life—and I like him.

[VAN ZORN, *who has been looking from time to time at the portrait over the piano, is now gazing at it with apparently unconscious intentness*]

VILLA

[*Glancing over her shoulder*]

Did you know *him*—my uncle?

VAN ZORN

[*Looking at her and shaking his head*]

I did not.

VILLA

My poor uncle Lovett was unfortunate, and I am glad for his sake that he is dead.   Does that sound hard?

VAN ZORN

Far from it.   I have known such cases.

VILLA

He died in this room.

VAN ZORN

I am not superstitious.

VILLA

He drank himself to death.

VAN ZORN

I am not uncharitable.

VILLA

He was a good man.

VAN ZORN

I have no doubt of it.

[*Pause*]

Lucas is a good man.

VILLA

[*Earnestly*]

He *is* good.   And I hope his meeting with you may prove to be fortunate.

VAN ZORN

[*Steadily*]

Lucas may prove to be the most fortunate of us all. Don't you think it would be well for at least one of us to be fortunate, even if the others are not?

VILLA

[*Half-frightened*]

The others?   You say such unexpected things.

VAN ZORN

[*Still with his hands on the back of the chair*]

Yes, the others.   The others who are not going to be fortunate.

VILLA

[*With a shrug*]

You speak like a wizard.   If you are trying to cast a spell over me, you might as well let me know beforehand.

[*Laughing thinly*]

All good wizards should do that, I think.

VAN ZORN

[*Firmly but rather sadly*]

I should say that the spell had already been cast.

VILLA

But what manner of spell do you mean?

[*Nervously*]

There are spells and spells, I suppose.   Aren't there?

VAN ZORN

I might say the spell that compels you to take so much apparent satisfaction in being insincere.

VILLA

[*Looking at him*]

Insincere?

VAN ZORN

[*Nods slowly*]

To yourself and to the others.   To the others who are not going to be fortunate.

VILLA

[*Biting her lip*]

Did you come to tell me this?

VAN ZORN

I came because I was called.   You may be surprised, but there is no reason why you should be offended.

VILLA

[*With a cold but artificial laugh*]

Amused, you mean.

VAN ZORN

[*Calmly and distinctly*]

No, that is not what I mean. For you cannot possibly find it amusing to know that you have the happiness of at least three lives at your disposal . . . Yes, in your power . . . Do you believe, really, that it would be amusing to make three new contributions to the world's unhappiness—much of which, from any finite point of view, is already unnecessary?

VILLA

[*Her lips tightening*]

I don't believe you realize what you are saying.

[*She rises*]

No, I don't mean that you are to go.

VILLA

[*She goes to the table and looks aimlessly at some objects that are on it*]

Will you tell me something?

VAN ZORN

[*Now at the right of the table, near the chair*]

Willingly, if I can.

VILLA

[*Toying with the broken paper cutter*]

What did you say to Weldon Farnham about—about this? And what did he say to you?

VAN ZORN

I asked him for one interview.

VILLA

And where do you intend to go at the end of this—one interview?

VAN ZORN

My own way, wherever that may lie.

[*Very distinctly*]

You may never see me again, but you will kindly believe me when I assure you that the situation before you is not—amusing.

VILLA

[*With half-hearted authority*]

Under ordinary conditions, you must see that I could not listen any longer to what you are saying.

VAN ZORN

I understand you perfectly.

[*Slowly, with a strange confidence*]

I understand at the same time that these are not ordinary conditions, and that you and I are not ordinary people.

VILLA

[*With a shrug*]

I am beginning to think that we are not.

[*With a reluctant smile*]

Do you think we are so very important?

VAN ZORN

[*With his hands on the back of the chair*]

Is anything important?

VILLA

[*Slowly*]

I wonder—sometimes.   And I thought

[*Rather feebly*]

that you were a friend of Weldon Farnham's.

VAN ZORN

His best friend, so far as I know.

VILLA

Does a man's best friend try to . . .

[*She stops as if frightened*]

VAN ZORN

Yes . . . If it is written so, yes.

VILLA

[*As if compelled*]

Do you mean—"destiny?"

VAN ZORN

You may give it whatever name you choose.   May I ask you another question?

VILLA

I suppose so.

[*With another shrug*]

But you needn't scare me.

VAN ZORN

[With a melancholy smile]

That is the last thing that I could possibly wish to do. What I have now to ask is this: Is it your unalterable will to deprive three people, including yourself, of the happiness that might as well be theirs?

VILLA

[Trying to laugh]

Why do you speak of my "will" and of your "destiny?" Mayn't I have a destiny as well as you?

VAN ZORN

[Looking at the portrait]

You have one undoubtedly.   And I have one interview.

[He stands as before with his hands on the back of the chair and watches her while she examines various objects on the table]

Are you sure that you know what it would mean if you were to make a mistake now?

[She gives him a bewildered look that is meant to be resentful, but he does not seem to notice it]

Are you sure that you are thinking of the years, and the darkness, and the long roads that lie in the darkness—and end there?   Are such things important, or are they still—amusing?

[VILLA stands looking vacantly at a picture post-card that is in her hand and finally turns the card towards VAN ZORN, speaking with a trace of injured and half-frightened humor in her voice and eyes]

VILLA
[*Irrelevantly*]

Did you ever see the Lion of Lucerne?

VAN ZORN
[*Suddenly inclined to laugh*]

No.

VILLA
[*Laughing*]

I thought you had seen everything.

VAN ZORN
[*Shaking his head slowly*]

I haven't. I have never seen you but once, until today.

VILLA
[*Laughing nervously*]

I don't see what the Lion of Lucerne has to do with your seeing me.

VAN ZORN
[*Smiling*]

I don't see what the Lion of Lucerne has to do with any of us.

[*He looks at the card and then at her, with the same melancholy and inquiring smile*]

I dare say that he has his good points.

VILLA
[*Throwing down the card and putting her hands behind her*]

I still think that I ought to be angry with you.

[*Ruefully*]

Every nerve and fibre tells me so.

VAN ZORN

You are too healthy to have nerves and fibres.   And
if you knew yourself better, you could not even think of
being angry with *me*.

VILLA
[With humor and self-assertion]

You are not an absolute mystery, and I know a great
deal about you, and about myself—that is, for a girl who
has never seen the Sphinx.

[Taking up the card again and looking at it]

I'll tell you something else that I know—something that
I've known for a long time.

[He nods slowly]

I have known for a long time that our ways,

[Quickly]

Weldon's way and mine, I mean,—have been leading us
just where you have said they are leading us—into the dark.

[Looking down]

And I have always been afraid of the dark.

[With a shrug and a laugh]

I wonder whether your coming to make me tell you this
may not be "destiny" after all.

VAN ZORN
[Looking at her fixedly]

There can be no doubt about that.

*[They stand looking at each other, she with her hands behind her,
    and he with his hands on the back of the chair. After a pause
    she turns quietly toward the door, where the maid is seen
    standing]*

THE MAID

Mr. Mink would like to see you, Miss Villa.

VILLA

[*Biting her lip to keep from laughing at* VAN ZORN'S *augmented solemnity*]

Tell him to come up, Jenny.

[*To* VAN ZORN]

You don't look as if you were going to be glad to see Otto. You ought to be, for he is a very nice boy.

VAN ZORN

[*Forcing a smile*]

So I have been told.

[OTTO *enters briskly, with a book in his hand. Being a child of nature he does not attempt to conceal his surprise at discovering* VAN ZORN *in the room*]

OTTO

[*Blankly*]

Oh! How do you do? . . . I'm afraid I'm in the way.

VILLA

[*Laughing*]

Of what, Otto? You foolish child, you are never in the way.

OTTO

[*Doubtfully*]

I don't know about that. But I have come, anyhow, as I said I would. And here, my adorable young lady,

is a copy of my latest abhorred twitterings.   Does it look
wicked?

VILLA

[Taking the book and laughing at OTTO*]*

It looks lovely. But why do you call it *Au Cinquième?*
You don't live on the fifth floor.

OTTO

[Briskly]

That isn't necessary. All you have to do is to shut
yourself up in almost any kind of place, have in a barrel
of mangoes, and let imagination do the rest.

VILLA

[Laughing]

Mangoes?

OTTO

[Cheerfully]

Mangoes. The mango has the flavor of all the fruits.
If you eat a barrel of 'em, you will have the wisdom of all
the ages.

[With a grimace]

Unhappily, I didn't eat my barrel quite fast enough, and
so I lost some of it.

VILLA

[Laughing]

That was too bad.

[Looking at the book]

But I hope the critics will be good to *Au Cinquième.*

OTTO

[Shaking his head sorrowfully]

They won't.

[Brightening]

Do you remember my last book—*Huitres et Chablis?*

[She nods and laughs]

Thank you for remembering it. Well,

[Putting his hands into his trousers pockets]

one inky-fingered imbecile advised me to write one more book as an antidote and to call it *Huile de Foie de Morue,* or Cod-liver-oil,—that being his private idea of humor. No, my dear young lady, Posterity is the only judge. Sometime, therefore, when I am gone—sometime when you are old and full of wrinkles—and rheumatism, if God wills it so—some far-off winter evening, for example, when you sit by the fire, with your cat in your lap,—say to yourself that Mink, who was always delicate, once took you out canoeing and contrived somehow to spill you into the beautiful Hudson, and that you swam ashore.

VILLA

And nearly died laughing.

OTTO

Oh, very well. But I can assure you both

[Looking at VAN ZORN, *who has been listening rather wearily]* that my neglected afflatus is of no manner of importance when compared with a bit of history that occurred about half an hour ago on Broadway, not far from Forty-second Street. It will do no good for me to tell it, for neither of you will believe it,—unless you believe in Noah's Ark, and such like.

VILLA

[*Quickly*]

We do believe in Noah's Ark, and you will please go on.
Sit down and tell us about it.

[*She sits on the piano stool*]

OTTO

I'd better not. I might not be able to get up again.
Well then, it's about Phœbus—Old Hundred—Lucas . . .
O Lord!

VAN ZORN

[*With a quick frown of inquiry*]

Has anything happened to Lucas?

OTTO

[*Looking from one to the other*]

It isn't easy to talk about.

VILLA

[*Impatiently*]

But tell me what you mean, Otto.

OTTO

I mean

[*Folding his arms*]

that Old Hundred has refused a gin-rickey.

VILLA

[*Forgetting herself*]

Oh! . . . But after all, was that so very wonderful?

[*Her manner reveals her suppressed excitement*]

OTTO

[*Innocently*]

You speak as if you thought so.

VILLA

[*More naturally*]

I spoke because I was glad.   It was the only thing for him to do, and I was afraid that he could never do it.

[*Eagerly again*]

Are you sure that he has done it, Otto,—or is this only once?

OTTO

[*With a queer smile of reminiscence*]

He has done it fast enough, if I know anything about him.

[*To* VAN ZORN, *with sudden expansion*]

You see, this friend of ours fills himself with fluid extract of early death for certain years, and then, all of a sudden, on Broadway, not far from Forty-second Street, he slaps a fellow kindly on the shoulder and tells a fellow that he, Phœbus, has been born again.   That was it,—"born again."

[*To* VILLA, *who has risen to her feet in her excitement*]

The man is illuminated, I tell you.   There is something in his eyes.

VAN ZORN

[*With tightening lips*]

Let us hope it is not dust.

OTTO

[*Standing on his toes*]

No, the dust is in *our* eyes, if anywhere.   Or it was.

VILLA

[*To* VAN ZORN, *gratefully*]

Not in *yours*, at any rate . . . And you have been the
cause of it all!

[OTTO *looks at* VAN ZORN *in amazement*]

VAN ZORN

[*As before*]

On the contrary, I don't know that I have ever been the
cause of anything.   But I agree with you in saying that
this was the only course for him to take, although I have
never shared your fear that he would not take it.

VILLA

[*Still wondering*]

But how did you know anything about him?

VAN ZORN

[*Smiling faintly*]

Oh, there are signs.   Moreover, I permitted Farnham
to tell me as much as he would about Lucas's early life.

VILLA

But he cannot possibly know much about it.

VAN ZORN

[*Thoughtfully*]

He spoke, I think, of an eccentric father.

[*He glances at the portrait of* LOVETT]

VILLA

Weldon was not here in those days and perhaps it was as well that he was not,—for he might not have understood.

[*As if to correct herself*]

I mean that men like Weldon find it hard to measure the importance of things that happen in other people's lives. They can't do otherwise, I suppose.

VAN ZORN

All of which being granted, there still remains no room for doubt as to Farnham's friendliness towards Lucas.

VILLA

[*Vexed*]

I didn't mean that. I don't see how I came to speak as I did.

OTTO

[*Going to* VILLA]

I'm very much afraid that you must put *me* down as the tender and innocent cause. Pardon my interruption, and—beware the book.

[*After a somewhat bewildered pause*]

Good afternoon.

VILLA

[*As he is going*]

Is there very much about Nineveh in it?

[*She laughs rather thinly*]

OTTO

[*With a grimace*]

Nineveh occurs but twice, and Babylon has disappeared entirely.

[*He bows with exaggerated deference and disappears*]

[*After* OTTO'S *departure there is a pause.* VILLA *sits down in the large chair at the left of the table, while* VAN ZORN *stands looking at the portrait. Both have become very serious, and* VILLA'S *voice and manner reveal more and more constraint and emotion during the following scene*]

VILLA

[*Trying to smile*]

What do you think of Otto, now?

[*Pause*]

Wasn't it strange—what he told us about George?

VAN ZORN

[*Standing near his chair*]

Was it any stranger than my coming to this house?

VILLA

[*Embarrassed*]

But your coming was different, and I knew just when to expect you.

VAN ZORN

Did you know just *why* you were to expect me?

VILLA

Well, no,—not quite.

VAN ZORN

Were you a little offended at my request to see you?

VILLA

[*Slowly*]

No.

VAN ZORN

You must at least have thought it very unusual.

VILLA

Possibly.

[*With a faint smile*]

But one looks for unusual things from you, somehow . . .
But I shouldn't have said that. I beg your pardon.

VAN ZORN

I am asking myself whether or not I should beg *your*
pardon.

VILLA

[*Her voice trembling*]

For telling me the truth?

VAN ZORN

No; but for remaining here when you must be wishing
that I would go away.

[*She pauses, rises quickly from her chair, and stands before him.
She can hardly control herself. He looks into her eyes and
then turns away*]

VILLA

[*Almost beseeching him*]

No, you must not do that! You must not go yet! ॰ . .
I can't let you go until I tell you something.

[*She moves back to her chair and sits down slowly*]

VAN ZORN

[*Unhappily, but with dignity*]

I don't wish you to tell me anything unless you are sure
that I should hear it; and I don't wish to take advantage
of your perplexity—or of your unhappiness. You will
understand that, I am sure; and you will agree with me,
no doubt, when I say that my position has already become
rather—well, say strange, to use your own word.

[*With unconscious bitterness*]

It will serve as well as another.

VILLA

[*Impulsively*]

I don't care how strange it is, or how strange you are,
so long as I know that I can trust you. If you were not
strange, I might not have the courage to ask you to help
me . . . I wonder if I ought to wait until I know you
better.

VAN ZORN

[*With deep feeling*]

You will never know me better, and I shall be always
at your service.

[*With a bitter smile*]

"They also serve who only stand and wait."

[*Pause*]

Even the blind can serve, in their limited way.

VILLA

[*Choking*]

You must not say that again. You must not . . .

[*Her voice breaks completely. She throws herself forward, laying her head and arms upon the table. Her whole body shakes, as if the prisoned emotion of years were finally asserting itself. VAN ZORN stands with his hands on the back of his chair and looks down at her with a great sorrow in his eyes. Finally he turns from her to the part of the table that is near him and absently picks up the pieces of ivory that LUCAS has broken*]

VAN ZORN

[*Fitting the pieces together, and speaking with difficulty*]

Then you are not going to Damascus, after all.

[VILLA'S *body still shakes with her emotion, and she makes no sign to show that she has heard him. He looks down at her as the curtain falls*]

CURTAIN

ACT III

ACT III

FARNHAM'S *studio, a little after ten in the evening. When the
curtain rises the room is dark, save for the light of the fire
which is now burning in the grate.*

FARNHAM *is lying stretched on the window seat. Presently he
gets up rather lazily, turns on the light, looks at his watch
and stands in the middle of the room with his hands thrust
deep into the pockets of a black velvet house coat. Apart
from this coat he is in evening dress. He moves about aimlessly, yawns, and takes a cigar from the box on the table.
As he is lighting it, the bell rings. He remains motionless
for a little while, and a strange hard smile comes over his face.
Finally, with a shrug of his shoulders he goes to the door and
admits* VAN ZORN, *who is dressed in ordinary business
clothes. His face wears a serious expression and he greets*
FARNHAM *with a kindly but somewhat uncanny smile.
Then he looks towards the portrait on the easel, which has
been moved back to its original place in Act I.*

FARNHAM
[Still smiling drily]

For such a demon of punctuality, it seems to me that
you are a bit late.

VAN ZORN
[Smiling as before]

Am I so insufferably punctual that I cannot have five
minutes' grace?

[He takes off his overcoat]

FARNHAM

[*Taking his coat and hat and putting them on the window seat*]

Oh, no offence.   You have made your own reputation.

[VAN ZORN *goes to the fire*]

Are you cold?

VAN ZORN

It's rather cool outside.

FARNHAM

[*With a grin*]

I noticed that when I came out of the subway.   Aren't you going to sit down?

VAN ZORN

Presently.

FARNHAM

Take your time about it.   Have a cigar.

[*He holds out the box and smiles*]

VAN ZORN

I'll take one later, if you don't mind.

FARNHAM

It's a Pedro.

VAN ZORN

Not now.

FARNHAM

[*Coaxingly*]

Colorado.

[VAN ZORN *shakes his head and smiles patiently*]

Very well.   Pardon me if I appear to urge you.

VAN ZORN

I can think of no one who should ask me to pardon him.

FARNHAM

You remind me of the noble Spaniard who had no enemies because he had killed them all.

VAN ZORN
[*Smiling faintly*]

I have never killed anybody, to my knowledge. I may once have had something to do with bringing a man back to life again.

FARNHAM

That was good. Did he thank you for it?

VAN ZORN

He didn't say very much.

FARNHAM

They don't as a rule, I believe. By the way,
[*Grinning*]
when do you intend to tackle Old Hundred?

VAN ZORN
[*Frowning slightly*]

I dined with Lucas this evening—if you mean Lucas.

FARNHAM
[*Surprised*]

Oho! You did?—Did he get drunk?

VAN ZORN

He did not.

FARNHAM

[Not too pleasantly]

Oh well, you needn't be discouraged over that. There'll be time enough between now and midnight.

VAN ZORN

[Distinctly]

There will be time enough between now and midnight for more things than you may have considered.

FARNHAM

[Puzzled]

I have no doubt of it. But no matter about Lucas. Tell me something more about your destiny.

[Drily]

How *is* your destiny this evening, anyway?

VAN ZORN

[Still standing by the fire]

My destiny is a very good destiny, but unfortunately it has encountered one that is better.—Unfortunately for myself I mean,—not in any sense for others.

FARNHAM

[Patronizingly]

You are a good fellow—altogether too good to be put at a disadvantage. But this once—only this once, upon my word—I can't help repeating that I didn't think much of it. One interview, and all that sort of thing. You see, it wasn't quite in your line.

[*Pause*]

Well, how much am I to know?—and how soon am I to know it?

[*Drily*]

Suppose you sit down in that chair.

[*Indicating the large chair*]

The consequent relaxation may be a good thing for you.

VAN ZORN

Thank you, I will.

[*He sits down and begins to drum with his fingers on the arms of the chair*]

FARNHAM

[*Sitting down*]

Now you look more comfortable.

VAN ZORN

[*Abruptly*]

I told you, Farnham, that I thought Lucas and I might possibly be of service to each other.

FARNHAM

[*Wearily*]

Can't you forget Lucas for the rest of this evening? Granting all his noble qualities—including his indefatigable industry—I don't yet understand that you came here to talk about him.

VAN ZORN
[*Earnestly*]

Farnham, if you had known what you were asking, you would never have asked me to forget Lucas this evening. I may forget my name, and my age, and my way to Forty-second Street, but I shall not be likely to forget Lucas this evening.

[*Pause*]

You told me this morning, I believe, that you had had enough of him for one day.

FARNHAM
[*Puzzled and irritated*]

Most assuredly I did, and I meant what I said. I'll be as glad as anybody if you can straighten him out, but what the devil sense is there in harping on him from morn till dewy eve? Why not let Lucas go for the present?

[*Becoming more incisive*]

You started out this afternoon, I believe, to acquire some very special information that doesn't seem to be forthcoming.

VAN ZORN
[*Slowly*]

It will come . . . And as for letting Lucas go—

FARNHAM
[*Throwing up his hands*]

Good God!

VAN ZORN
[*Calmly*]

—letting Lucas go will be very difficult. In fact, it

will be out of the question. Instead of letting Lucas go, I fear that we shall be under the necessity of letting Lucas come.

FARNHAM

[*Unpleasantly*]

What are you talking about? I didn't ask him to come, did I?

VAN ZORN

[*As before*]

You did not, and *I* did not.

[*Drumming with his fingers*]

But he is coming all the same. I have no doubt that he has been coming—through the ages.

FARNHAM

[*Laughing drily*]

So that's it. More of your infernal Destiny, I suppose.

VAN ZORN

[*Earnestly*]

Whatever you do, Farnham, you had better wait a while before you begin to find fault with Destiny. For I should be inclined to say that you are going to be far more fortunate than I am, or am ever likely to be.

[*He looks thoughtfully about the studio*]

FARNHAM

Oh, you needn't try to smooth it over like that. I only meant that I was looking forward to this evening for a different kind of talk from this.

VAN ZORN
[*Quietly*]

You will have it yet.

FARNHAM
[*Wearily*]

With Lucas?

VAN ZORN
[*With deliberation*]

Farnham, if I don't give you certain information that you have every reason to expect, it is because I don't feel that I am in a position to give it. But I will say,
[*Smiling*]
at the risk of my life, that Lucas has been straightened out. I don't know just how I know it, but I know it.
[*With another smile*]
Your engaging friend Otto brought the news this afternoon—
[*Casually*]
not long after Lucas left Mrs. Lovett's house.

FARNHAM
[*Rising and speaking sharply*]

Lucas at Mrs Lovett's house? . . . You are keeping something back from me, and I should like very much to know what it is.

VAN ZORN
[*Reluctantly*]

Yes, I am keeping something back. And I have something else that I was requested, and finally persuaded, to give to you this evening. I would rather not do it, but it may be as well that I should.

FARNHAM

[*With dry fervor*]

I hope it will be something more tangible than what you have been giving me.

VAN ZORN

[*Giving him a small object*]

There it is.

FARNHAM

[*After a stupefied pause*]

Man alive, are you out of your senses? This is Villa Vannevar's ring. What the devil has been going on?

[*Sharply*]

Why don't you tell me?

VAN ZORN

Miss Vannevar will do that.

[FARNHAM *scowls incredulously*]

She and Lucas have been together, at her special request, since eight o'clock. Until she comes, please remember that I am acting only as a messenger.

FARNHAM

[*Looking from the ring to* VAN ZORN]

Are you all trying to make a fool of me? Are you the

friend that I have been trusting and praising all these years?

[*With a falling inflection*]

I'd better build a cabin in the woods . . . What does all this insanity mean, anyhow? You can answer that question, if you have a mind to, and you know it damned well.

VAN ZORN

[*Quietly*]

Farnham.

[*Pause*]

You are going to have two more visitors this evening, and they are nearly due. They are not going to stay, in all probability, more than fifteen minutes. When they are gone, you and I may have something more to say to each other.

FARNHAM

That is altogether possible.

VAN ZORN

[*Rising*]

And if I have been the indirect means of this sudden change in the course of events, I wish you to know that I believe, as I stand here, that events would have taken the same course, though not quite so suddenly, if I had never gone to Mrs. Lovett's house this afternoon. I mean, you understand, so far as events concern you personally. So be a good fellow and try to keep a little of your old faith in me.

[*Pause*]

Do you hear a motor coming?

[*He takes out his watch and smiles wearily at* FARNHAM]
They are on time, if I was not.

[*The bell rings.* FARNHAM *admits* LUCAS *and* VILLA VANNEVAR. LUCAS *has more color in his face, and his eyes are brighter than in the morning. He carries himself through the following scene with far more dignity and ease than might be expected, with now and then a facial suggestion of appreciative humor. Of the two* VILLA *is the more excited, but hers is the excitement of determination rather than of embarrassment or fear*]

FARNHAM

[*To the three, after rather formal greetings to* LUCAS *and* VILLA]
Well, I have the honor to report that I am still in the dark.

[*With a hard smile*]
Won't you all sit down?

[*They remain standing*]

VILLA

[*Going to* FARNHAM *and speaking with suppressed excitement*]
Oh, but I am glad to hear you say that—that you are in the dark.

[*He nods with condescension and she steps back a little*]
I was afraid you didn't know it.

[*Pause*]
Weldon, do you know what it was doing to me? But you don't, because you can't. I shall have to tell you what it was doing. It was driving me mad.

FARNHAM

[*Drily, with a glance at* LUCAS]
Kindly go on.

VILLA

It was killing me.

[FARNHAM *nods again*]

I know you are going to think some dreadful things about me,—and say them too, I suppose.

[*Rapidly*]

But whatever you do or say, don't ever forget that I am the cause of all that's happened this evening. I took the matter into my own hands—just because I couldn't wait. And when my mind was once made up that I couldn't wait,—well, I couldn't wait.

[*He nods again*]

And I couldn't see much need of spending days and nights in talking about it.

FARNHAM

[*With a shrug, and another look at* LUCAS]

Naturally not.

VILLA

[*To* VAN ZORN, *who is standing near the fire*]

And you

[*Gratefully but rapidly*]

—you remember what I told you when I got over that foolish fit of crying. I told you that nothing could ever make me change, and I asked you to help me. You told me first that you would rather not, and you said something that I didn't hear about circumstances; but finally you did agree to do a little—just because you could see that I was so much in earnest—and that nothing could ever make me change—and that I couldn't wait.

[VAN ZORN *replies with a slow nod, and* FARNHAM *grins at* LUCAS *with sardonic incredulity*]

FARNHAM

[*To* VILLA, *with a dry laugh*]

Will you be so kind as to let me know what this thing is or was,—you haven't yet given it a name—that was driving you mad, and killing you, and whatever else it may have been doing? You don't look to me like a dying person, as you stand there now.

VILLA

[*Impatiently*]

Oh, you know what it was. It was our horribly false position—pretending to care for each other when we didn't—I mean when we didn't care enough.

FARNHAM

[*Unpleasantly*]

In that case, perhaps you will be good enough to tell me what sort of position you would call this that we are in now.

[*He looks at* LUCAS *and* VAN ZORN]

Lucas, why do you stand there like that? Why don't you say something—if you have anything to say?

VILLA

[*Quickly, looking from* LUCAS *to* FARNHAM]

He can't speak yet, for I shan't let him. I shan't let anybody speak until I have said what I have to say. No, not one of you three can say a word until I tell you that I have asked George Lucas to marry me.

[FARNHAM *and* VAN ZORN *are almost equally surprised at this announcement, though the latter quickly regains his usual composure.* LUCAS *looks at first as if he would like to get away, but endures his unlooked-for prominence with an Indian-like resignation*]

There!

[*With her hands behind her back*]

Now you may all speak at once, if you care to.

FARNHAM

[*Going to* VILLA, *after a pause, and taking one of her hands*]

Villa, what is the matter with you this evening? Has the moon driven you insane?

[*To* LUCAS, *sharply*]

Lucas, why don't you say something?

LUCAS

[*With a dry cough*]

You are quite right. The time has come for me to speak.

FARNHAM

Well, if the time has come for you to speak, why the devil don't you?

LUCAS

[*Calmly, but uncomfortably and with several oratorical pauses*]

I am going to say something—and I don't see how it is going to take me very long to say it.

[*With another cough*]

Knowing—as I need hardly tell you now—that I could not, in view of my past and present circumstances—presume to ask of this lady the kind of question that she has taken upon herself to ask of me—and this time without wholly

anticipating its immediate effect upon one's nervous
organization,—well, I can only say that she has acted in
accordance with her own convictions in regard to the solution of a rather difficult problem, and has thereby placed
me under excessive obligations—that she cannot expect
ever to be entirely fulfilled.

[*To* FARNHAM, *with a faint smile*]

Whatever else you may wish me to say will be related,
with your permission, at another time.

FARNHAM

[*With cold humor*]

"She has acted in accordance with her own convictions
in regard to the solution of a rather difficult problem."

[*To* VAN ZORN, *drily*]

As she sees it, I suppose.

VAN ZORN

Is there more than one way to see it?

FARNHAM

I see it as a bit of impetuous farce.

VILLA

[*Protesting violently*]

No, don't say impetuous. Say anything but that. Say
determined —ordained— premeditated— desperate—anything but impetuous. I'll not have anybody—not even
George—tell me that I was impetuous when I was only
sensible. You might as well call me—I don't know what.
You might as well call me a fool.

FARNHAM

[*With reluctant humor*]

Do you know, my dear young lady, that you are using some rather positive language?

VILLA

[*Still excited*]

I don't care. I must use it, in order to make myself understood.

[*To* LUCAS]

Tell him, George, about the ring.

FARNHAM

[*Satirically*]

Yes, George, let us hear about the ring.

LUCAS

She means that the ring would have been returned to you in any case.

FARNHAM

[*To* VAN ZORN, *with fine irony*]

And this is your work.

VAN ZORN

[*Distinctly*]

No, my friend, you are mistaken. It is not the work of any human being—in this room, or out of it.

FARNHAM

[*Wearily*]

Oh, the devil! I've heard all that before.

[VAN ZORN *shrugs his shoulders and looks at the fire*]

VILLA

[*Earnestly*]

Weldon, let me tell you again what I told you when I came in.

[*With intensity*]

It was killing me.   It was driving me mad.

FARNHAM

[*Throwing up his hands*]

For heaven's sake, are you going to drag that nonsense in again?

VILLA

It meant the torture of our two lives . . . The ruin of them, for all we know.

FARNHAM

[*With a careless absence of emotion*]

Lives are not so easily ruined as all that.   If they were, some of us would be ruined before we were born.

VAN ZORN

[*With a faint smile*]

Some of us are, Farnham.

FARNHAM

[*To* VAN ZORN, *with hesitation*]

Don't you think that you have contributed about enough to the needless absurdity and injustice of all this . . .

VILLA

[*Quickly*]

No, you must not say that to him.   It was I who did

this, and it was I who insisted that it should be done to-night. If your best friend had not helped me, I should have done it sooner or later without him . . . Now will you let me go on from where I was when you interrupted me?

FARNHAM
[*With evident admiration*]

Yes, if you remember where that was.

VILLA
[*With animation*]

It was where I was going to say something more about George.

[FARNHAM *looks at* LUCAS, *who is looking at the bust of Shakespeare*]

Weldon, there are certain people in this world who are made for each other. You may laugh at me for saying so—I know it isn't very original—but I believe it to be true, and that makes it just the same as if it *were* true. Well then, I believe that George Lucas and I have belonged to each other since the beginning of our lives, and I have known it ever since I can remember. I knew him long before I knew you, and I know more about him than you have ever known or ever can know;

[FARNHAM *looks again at* LUCAS]

and once, when I was so scared and happy that I didn't know what to do—this was ages ago—I told Auntie all about it.
[*With comical directness*]

Auntie didn't like—his father.

FARNHAM
[With venomous humor]

And what did Auntie say?

VILLA
[With a shrug and a rueful laugh]

Oh dear! If I were to try to tell you what she said, I shouldn't know how to begin or where to end. It doesn't make so much difference what Auntie said, so long as she said—what she said.

[With unconscious humor, looking down]

She didn't like George's father.

FARNHAM
[Grinning at LUCAS]

Did she like George?

[Pause]

George doesn't seem to have anything more to say.

LUCAS
[With dry emphasis]

Yes, George has one thing more to say. He has to say that he has not yet accepted the lady's offer.

FARNHAM
[Scowling]

Then why are you here?

LUCAS

To do so in your presence—now that you understand the situation.

FARNHAM

But I don't understand the situation—except in the vaguest kind of way . . . I knew about it in that way before.

VAN ZORN

[*Still standing by the fire*]

Farnham, I don't like to interrupt you.

FARNHAM

Oh—you don't . . .

VAN ZORN

But why debate the inevitable? It will do no manner of good, and it will be likely, as Miss Vannevar has already implied, to take up a great deal of time.

FARNHAM

[*Drily*]

Have you been coaching them?

[VAN ZORN *makes a gesture of resigned protest, but says nothing*]

Well, you haven't told me what you said to Lucas during dinner.

VAN ZORN

I told Lucas that Miss Vannevar wished very much to see him as soon as possible after eight o'clock.

FARNHAM

Was that all?

VAN ZORN

Substantially, yes.

FARNHAM

Mightn't that leave a pretty wide margin for conjecture?

VAN ZORN

It might, but it doesn't. Please remember that when I told you of my interest in Lucas, I was not anticipating the developments that have transpired.

FARNHAM

[*Unwilling to let the subject go*]

But you are the cause of these developments, for all that. What did you say to Villa after Otto went away?

VAN ZORN

[*With a slight weariness*]

I didn't find a great deal to say. I told her pretty much what I have told you,—that Lucas and I were going to be of service to each other, and that I had complete confidence in him. Please do not ask me to go any further into details—just now.

[*With a friendly smile*]

My dear Farnham, if you were to form at your time of life the fatal habit of clinging to ruins, and of refusing to accept what has irrevocably taken place, there is no knowing what might happen to you—and to your art.

FARNHAM

Do you remember that you used to call yourself a friend of mine?

[*He speaks half-heartedly, and seems to regret having spoken*]

VAN ZORN
[*Distinctly*]

I was never in my life more convinced of my complete
loyalty to you, or of your complete faith in me. I was not
expecting to say so this evening, unless to you alone, but
never mind that now.

FARNHAM
[*Rather ruefully*]

I suppose that's your fantastic, esoteric, oriental way
of telling a fellow that he has said something foolish. I
don't say it's a bad way, you understand—

[*He stops, and has another look at* LUCAS, *who smiles in approval*]

VILLA
[*Going to* FARNHAM *and putting her hands on his arms*]

You needn't try to be angry any longer, for I can see by
the look in your eyes that you can't.

[*Shaking him a little and beginning to laugh*]

You ought not to be angry, for you are so glad to get rid
of me that you don't know what to do with yourself.
You may tell me that I ought not to say so, but you can't
put the words back into my mouth—'cause I've got my
teeth together.

[*She shows her teeth and laughs at him*]

FARNHAM
[*Taking her hands and smiling*]

I don't remember having said that I was angry.

[*He pushes her away gently*]

VILLA

[*Putting her hands behind her and laughing*]

There was no need of your *saying* it.

FARNHAM

[*Drily*]

Then that must have been the reason why I didn't say it.

[*Pause*]

But don't you think that I had just the slightest conceivable reason for being—for being a trifle annoyed, we'll say?

VILLA

[*With feline demureness*]

Well, I rather suppose you did.

[*Looking at him brightly*]

But it's all over now, *isn't* it?

FARNHAM

[*Trying not to laugh*]

And so you find your escape from me a very simple matter.

[*With mild sarcasm*]

It seems to be one of the prerogatives of womankind to discover now and then that some problems *are* very simple.

VILLA

[*She looks at* LUCAS, *then for a longer time at* VAN ZORN, *who still remains by the fire, and finally at* FARNHAM *again*]

And that others are very difficult.

[FARNHAM *glances at* VAN ZORN, *who stands looking at the burning coals. There is a pause, which is broken by the ringing of the bell.* FARNHAM *admits* OTTO, *who stands for a time in meek bewilderment after looking from one to the other*]

OTTO

I—I saw the light, and so I came over—from Pethrick's.

FARNHAM
[*Drily amused*]

Of course you did, Otto. That was the right thing for you to do. We have all seen the light, even if we haven't all come over from Pethrick's.
[*Patting his shoulder*]
Now take a look around you, little friend, and tell us what you see besides the light.

OTTO
[*Looking from* LUCAS *to* VILLA]

Oh—good evening.
[*He plays with his hat*]
I saw the light, and so I came over.
[*To* LUCAS] \
Did you see the light, Phœbus, and did you come over?

LUCAS
[*Avoiding over-confidence*]

Yes, Otto, I may be said to have seen the light, and to have come over—though not from Pethrick's.

OTTO
[*With a long sigh*]
That's illuminating, and I thank you kindly.

[*He looks at* Van Zorn, *who smiles and nods*]

Good evening.

[*To* Villa]

Are you sure that I'm not in the way?

[*He makes a puzzled grimace and looks at* Farnham, *who grins*]

VILLA
[*Laughing nervously*]

We are sure of one thing, Otto, and that is that you are not very cordial with your old friends. Aren't you going to congratulate me on my engagement to George Lucas? We are going to be married—sometime.

OTTO
[*After a stupefied pause*]

Are you?

[*He looks again from one to another, and finally addresses* Van Zorn]

I knew this afternoon that something was going to happen. Of course it was none of my business, but you—you understand me, I'm sure.

[*He wipes his forehead with his handkerchief*]

FARNHAM
[*With lingering sarcasm*]

We understand you, Otto. You saw the light and you came over. Everything has been explained, and we are all going to try to be happy.

OTTO
[*Looking again from one to another, and beginning to beam*]

Do you know, Farnham, that I—that I rather like this?

FARNHAM

I'm glad to hear you say so, Otto. We study to please.

OTTO

[*To* VAN ZORN, *who appears to be mildly amused*]
Do *you* like this?

VAN ZORN

It has my unqualified approval. In addition, it was undoubtedly inevitable.

OTTO

[*With an air of discovery*]
Doesn't that make it all the better?

VAN ZORN

I am sure that you have every reason to congratulate your friends on their mutual good fortune.

OTTO

[*After shaking hands, rather suddenly, with* VILLA *and* LUCAS]
Farnham, old man, the more I think of this, the better I like it. There's a—there's a kind of destiny about it.

FARNHAM

[*Patting Otto's shoulder*]
Otto, we can always look to you for the right word.
[*Wearily, with a mild trace of venom*]
I've been trying to think of that word "destiny" all the evening.

VILLA

[*Giving* FARNHAM *her hand*]

And I have been trying to think of something more to say to *you*, Weldon, but somehow I can't just now. So I think George had better take me home. And then, I suppose I'll have a talk with . . .

[*She sighs*]

FARNHAM

[*With an unfeeling grin*]

With Auntie?

VILLA

Yes, with Auntie.

[*She breaks into childish laughter*]

Poor Auntie!

[*Pause*]

Well, good night. I won't say good-bye, for that would be too solemn.

FARNHAM

[*Holding her hand*]

Good night. And I hope you will be very happy.

[*Shaking hands with* LUCAS]

Good night, George,—and my congratulations. You will excuse me if I don't make a speech.

VILLA

[*To* VAN ZORN, *who comes forward*]

Good night.

[*She gives him her hand and looks at him as if a little frightened*]

VAN ZORN

[*Holding her hand*]

Good night.

[*They look into each other's eyes for some time. She leaves him slowly and moves towards the door. He returns to his former place by the fire, after speaking with* LUCAS]

VILLA

[*While* LUCAS *is shaking hands with* VAN ZORN]

Good night, Otto.

OTTO

[*Still bewildered*]

Good night. I don't think I'll make a speech either. On the contrary I may as well go home to my mousy garret, light my guttering candle, and work away for a while at my popular song.

VILLA

[*Laughing*]

But you never told me that you were writing a popular song. How does it go, and what is it about?

OTTO

[*Solemnly*]

It's a sad story, and it doesn't go very fast.

[*Doubtfully*]

And it may not be altogether appropriate to the present auspicious occasion.

VILLA

[*Laughing*]

Oh, yes it is—perfectly. How does it go, Otto?

OTTO

[Scratching his ear thoughtfully]

I've only got four lines of it.

[He appears to be reading them from the inside of his hat]

VILLA

[Shaking him]

But how do they go?

OTTO

They go like this:

[He repeats the following lines with comical solemnity, punctuating them with sharp pauses]

Oh, long shall we remember the dark days that followed then,

And how our faith in truth and honor sank;

For we knew the dear old home would never be the same again,

When Father robbed the baby's little bank.

LUCAS

[Laughing]

Can you keep it up to that level, Otto?

OTTO

[Scratching his ear]

I think so.

[With owlish innocence]

But of course you understand that there's nothing prophetic about it—nothing personal. I wouldn't have any words of mine cast a shadow on this propitious hour—no, not even if my friend Farnham were to give me a small potion of his Double X Rattlesnake Rye over yonder.

[*He nods towards the bust of Shakespeare*]

I'm delicate, and I may not be with you very long.

VILLA

[*To* FARNHAM, *laughing*]

Before you give it to him, I think it will be safer for me to go away. Good night again.

[FARNHAM *goes with* VILLA *and* LUCAS *to the vestibule, closing the door slowly and thoughtfully as he returns.* OTTO, *in the meantime, has gone to the cabinet, from the depths of which he has produced a bottle of whiskey.* VAN ZORN, *standing by the fire, watches* OTTO *with a look of abstracted amusement.*]

FARNHAM

[*Returning*]

Well, Otto, you seem to be in a romantic frame of mind this evening. You aren't unhappy, are you?

OTTO

[*Wiping his lips*]

No, I don't complain.

FARNHAM

[*Patronizingly, to Van* ZORN]

Otto never complains. He eats his crust at sunset, and he drains his cup of bitterness without so much as making a face. Don't you, Otto?

OTTO

[*Moving towards the door*]

Don't ask me to talk this evening. You have shaken me up, and I'm delicate. I may be on my way to eminence, or I may be merely another case of the gods seeing otherwise. In either event, it will be all right, for the universe will take care of us all. Throw on my grave a flower. Fare you well, gentlemen both, and peace be with you.

[OTTO *lays his hand on his heart, bows deferentially, and disappears slowly and silently*]

VAN ZORN

[*Smiling faintly*]

You must not undervalue that youth, Farnham.

FARNHAM

[*Opening the cigar-box*]

I shall never again undervalue anything that has a destiny.

[*Holding out the box*]

Here—have a cigar. And for God's sake have it this time or you'll make me peevish.

VAN ZORN

Thank you.

[*He takes a match from Farnham and lights his cigar*]

FARNHAM

[*Lighting his cigar*]

I suppose Otto has a destiny, hasn't he?

VAN ZORN
[*Drily*]

I suppose he has.

FARNHAM
[*Giving him a queer look*]

And what about Lucas—and *his* destiny?
[*He sits down and invites* VAN ZORN *to take the large chair as before*]

VAN ZORN
[*Calmly*]

I don't know that I pretend to be a prophet,
[FARNHAM *grins*]
but I should venture to say that Lucas's destiny will not be altogether a bad one. Being human and not a fool, he must in the nature of things have ambitions that he will never realize. On the other hand, he will have a great deal of happiness, I believe.
[*Looking earnestly at* FARNHAM]
But neither he nor I can have what *you* are going to have.
[FARNHAM *begins to beam with approval and anticipation*]
I won't say that you have it already
[*He glances toward the picture and scowls*]
—for that might not be good for you . . . and it might not be true.

FARNHAM
[*Affecting modesty*]

You may be within a gunshot of being right, but this day's work doesn't seem to be very promising—that is, to the uninitiated.

[Clasping his knee]

I suppose, however, that *you* feel a great deal better.

VAN ZORN

Why do you say that?

FARNHAM

After what you have done?

VAN ZORN
[With a frown]

I have done nothing. I thought that was understood.

FARNHAM
[Laughing a little]

Oh yes, you have, in spite of your cosmic modesty. Haven't you cleared the air? Haven't you raised the curtain?

VAN ZORN
[Apparently after some hesitation]

Would you talk like that, Farnham, if you knew me a little better . . . if you knew, as I know, what I have lost?

FARNHAM
[With a trace of his old manner]

We have things before we lose them. That's old, I know; but I believe it's true.

VAN ZORN
[More earnestly]

Yes, Farnham, it is quite true. And it is most distinctly what I have had that I have now lost.

FARNHAM
[*Puzzled*]

Go on. You are talking; I'm only listening.

VAN ZORN
[*Very distinctly*]

What is your notion of the best thing for a man to do when he has lost his belief that he has something to live for?

FARNHAM
[*Pretending not to understand*]

Why, that's easy. Find something new to live for.

VAN ZORN
[*Getting up and speaking as if half to himself*]

There may be a certain amount of wisdom in that. And yet you do not wholly understand me.

FARNHAM
[*With unconscious emphasis*]

And who the devil does?

VAN ZORN
[*Looking steadily at* FARNHAM]

Do you know what it is, Farnham, that I am facing?

FARNHAM
[*With a forced laugh*]

You are facing *me*, for the moment. I'm not much to be facing, I grant you; but you might have to face something worse.

[*With a glance at the picture*]

The deadliest thing about me, at present, seems to be my ability to paint pictures like that one over there.

VAN ZORN

[*Becoming more and more serious*]

I seem to be facing you, Farnham, but the truth is that I am facing myself. Whichever way I look now, I look forward into a thousand mirrors; and I see myself—only myself—Van Zorn. If I had one talent, I should see that; and I should thank God for it. But it isn't there. There is nothing there but—Van Zorn.

[*He smokes for a time in thought*]

Farnham, do you wonder that there are people in this world who howl about property? . . . Yes; my property, if you like.

FARNHAM

[*Laughing*]

Good! That sounds as if the yeast were beginning to work. You needn't worry; you'll find something to live for.

[*Getting up and stretching himself comfortably*]

Why don't you begin by tearing down a row of rotten tenements—just for the fun of it—and putting up some thing—oh, something sanitary and ornamental? Then the tired father could come home and cleanse his honest hide in a white enameled bath-tub—only of course he wouldn't,—and after dinner the entire family could sit around a gilded radiator and sing songs by the most eminent composers, as Otto would say, of their native land.

[Laughing]

Hear me, Norma, but don't excite yourself. You are still young, and there's going to be no end of time.

VAN ZORN

[With a dutiful smile]

There is something in what you say.

FARNHAM

[With easy patronage]

You bet there is. And then there is always this "business" of yours: "Van Zorn and Lucas, the eminent comedians." Don't you see *that*, when you look forward into your thousand mirrors?

VAN ZORN

[Looking down]

Yes, I see it. The business will succeed.

FARNHAM

To be sure.

[Becoming over-confident]

Van Zorn, from whom all blessings flow, do you realize that we are beaten by Old Hundred?

VAN ZORN

[Gravely]

I don't like your word—beaten.

FARNHAM

[Piqued but persistent]

Neither do I,—but I didn't invent it, and I won't say it

again. But I should like to ask you one question. When you came in this evening, you said something about your destiny being a very good destiny; and you said, also, that it had encountered—I think that was your word—one that was better. Now, if I have a right to ask the question, I wish you would be good enough to tell me what the devil Lucas was doing this afternoon at Mrs. Lovett's.

VAN ZORN

He came to tell Miss Vannevar that he was going west, and to say good-bye.

FARNHAM

Going west—eh?

[*Excited but satirical*]

And if you hadn't kept Lucas from going west—whatever that means—I suppose you would have been contented for all time with your—your one interview.

VAN ZORN

[*After some deliberation*]

If Lucas had gone—west,—you would still have re-covered your ring.

[*They look at each other until Farnham shrugs his shoulders and looks at the floor*]

When Lucas changed his mind about going, he was not in any manner influenced by the ring or by the person who wore it.

[*Pause*]

But why say more about that?

[*His last words come rather thickly; he moves away and finally remains standing before the picture*]

By the way, Farnham, what are you going to do with this picture?

FARNHAM
[*Drily*]

You speak as if you wanted it yourself.

VAN ZORN

Will you give it to me?

[*He is evidently in earnest*]

FARNHAM
[*Cynically*]

Yes, take it. Take everything in sight.

VAN ZORN
[*Thoughtfully*]

I could almost believe that this picture was painted for me—without your knowledge.

FARNHAM
[*Drily*]

More destiny?

VAN ZORN
[*Taking a small knife from his pocket*]

I don't know what else to call it.

[*He begins to cut the head and shoulders from the canvas*]

FARNHAM
[*Going quickly towards him*]

Here! What do you think you are doing?

VAN ZORN

[*Cutting diligently*]

I am getting rid of one of the most insincere

[*Cuts*]

and exasperating

[*Cuts*]

bits of charlatanry

[*Cuts*]

that man's eyes have ever looked on. I am doing it partly for the good of your artistic conscience, and partly for reasons of my own.

FARNHAM

[*Unable to protest*]

All right, the thing is yours.

[*With cynical observation*]

But I suppose you know that you are disintegrating twenty-five hundred dollars worth of high art?

VAN ZORN

[*Throwing the piece of canvas into the fire*]

Is that your figure?

FARNHAM

For the present, yes. And therefore it seems to me that your eccentric little ingle-flame over there is just a bit extravagant.

VAN ZORN

[*Punching the burning canvas with the poker*]

I shouldn't worry about that if I were you. We are living in an extravagant age.

[*He puts away the poker and stands watching the fire. At length he turns to* FARNHAM *and speaks with a subdued intensity and a new emphasis*]

It is your age, Farnham, and you had better not play with it.

[*Slowly*]

If I were you, I should try to meet it half way.

[VAN ZORN *throws his cigar into the fire and stands looking at the smouldering canvas, holding his hands behind him.* FARNHAM *goes toward him slowly, holds out his hand and looks for a moment into* VAN ZORN'S *eyes.* VAN ZORN *takes his hand, lets it go, and continues to look down into the fire*]

FARNHAM

[*Embarrassed and with evident regret*]

I'm sorry, old fellow, but I didn't quite . . . I didn't realize that you were quite so much in earnest.

[VAN ZORN *makes no reply, but remains looking at the fire.* FARNHAM *sits down on the edge of the window-seat and looks thoughtfully at the floor before him. Finally he looks again at Van Zorn, and a slow incredulous smile comes over his face. Then he shrugs his shoulders, as if he was still in doubt about something, and the curtain falls slowly.*]

THE END